Inside China

*Endpapers : The Royal Lady of the East
greets the Royal Lord of the West
Previous page and chapter openings :
Rubbings from ancient Chinese tombs showing
aspects of daily life and the seven famous horses of Mu Wang,
5th King of the Zhou Dynasty, 1001–746 BC*

Inside China

BY THE RIGHT HONOURABLE

Malcolm MacDonald

O.M.

WITH PHOTOGRAPHS BY

William MacQuitty

Heinemann · London

DEDICATED TO
The Great Britain – China Centre
which helps a great deal to promote
friendly co-operation between the peoples of
the British and the Chinese nations.

DESIGNED AND PICTURE-EDITED BY
CRAIG DODD

William Heinemann Ltd
10 Upper Grosvenor Street London W1X 9PA

LONDON MELBOURNE TORONTO
JOHANNESBURG AUCKLAND

First published 1980

ISBN 434 44040 X

Printed and bound in Great Britain by
Fakenham Press Limited, Fakenham, Norfolk

Contents

I wish to thank my old friend Malcolm MacDonald for sparing his valuable time to write about the country and people we have both known and admired for half a century. My thanks are also due to Miss Elizabeth Wright, Director of the Great Britain-China Centre and to Miss Penny Brooke, its Deputy Director, for checking the captions.

I thank my wife, Betty MacQuitty, for her unfailing help. As with my other books several of her photographs appear in *Inside China*. During our visits to China we received efficient and courteous help from Luxingshe, the China Travel Service, and were greeted with unfailing interest and enthusiasm in Universities, communes, hospitals, schools·and factories; indeed everywhere we went.

I also record my appreciation of the Standard Chartered Bank in whose service I achieved my earliest ambition of working in China.

Finally my thanks to my talented friend Craig Dodd who selected the photographs from my collection and designed the book; the fifth on which we have worked together.

WILLIAM MACQUITTY

Foreword

THIS IS A BRIEF NARRATIVE OF THE EVENTS WHICH LED TO THE CREATION OF THE PEOPLE'S
Republic of China in 1949, and of what has developed there since. It is not a scholarly
account of that extremely important piece of modern history based on erudite researches
into all the relevant official documents and other sources of information. A more
amateur piece of work, it is mostly a report by a traveller in China on what he observed
there during periodic visits. I had the good fortune to go there in 1929, 1948, 1962,
1971, 1975 and 1979, and on each occasion I was able to journey quite widely through
various parts of the vast land. I have therefore been able to catch glimpses of the
remarkable changes which have taken place in it during the last half century, and
especially since Mao Zedong (Mao Tse-tung) and his comrades gained power throughout
mainland China thirty years ago. Moreover, I was able not only to see with my own
eyes many features of the developing scene but also to hear with my own ears the
opinions of many types of Chinese people, from numerous humble folk to some of
their most eminent leaders, about what was happening there.

A fully comprehensive, adequately detailed account of every important aspect of
the transformation would, of course, fill several volumes. In this single rather short
one I have had to omit references to many interesting matters, making it a sketch of the
main significant changes which have occurred in Chinese society and in its government's outlook on international affairs. I have attempted to bring the picture up to
date to the end of 1979.

My written descriptions are brought vividly to life by the brilliant pictures taken
by William MacQuitty, a photographer of genius. He and I have endeavoured to
produce a book which will catch the attention of members of the general reading
public, because it is important that they gain knowledge and understanding of what
is now happening in the re-emerging great Chinese nation.

For almost all the names of Chinese people and places I have used the modern
Chinese spelling (putting the old spelling in a bracket after the first reference to each
one). An index at the end of the book also contains the two spellings, for the con-
venience of readers.

I am very grateful to three authorities on contemporary China – Sir John Addis, one
of our recent British Ambassadors there, Miss Elizabeth Wright, the Director of the
Great Britain–China Centre, and Miss Penny Brooke, its Deputy Director – for reading
through an earlier draft of my text and suggesting various good amendments to what I
had written.

MALCOLM MACDONALD

1 The End of Imperial China

MANY VERY SIGNIFICANT POLITICAL CHANGES HAVE OCCURRED IN THE WORLD DURING the last half-century. The disintegration of the overseas empires of the old European powers, the emergence of the United States of America and Soviet Russia as the two super-powers, the transformation of about forty of Britain's former dependent colonies into a Commonwealth of independent nations, the creation of the massive United Nations Organization in succession to the much more limited League of Nations, and the establishment of the European Community are a few of them. As important as any is the re-emergence of a strong China. The rest of mankind is beginning to wake up to the potentially titanic nature of that event.

The strength of China does not spring only from the fact that the Chinese now number more than 950,000,000 people, nearly a quarter of the world's total population. It is their excellent quality combined with their massive quantity that makes them so extremely important. They are as physically energetic, intellectually able and culturally gifted as any race of human beings around the Earth.

The story of their progress from remote prehistoric times onwards makes a fascinating narrative. Recently excavated fossilized bits and pieces of their antique ancestors reveal that a type of man lived in China at least 1,700,000 years ago; and many surviving fragments of their recorded history, like inscribed oracle bones, show that a maturely civilized society already flourished in widespread parts of the land almost 4,000 years ago.

One of the remarkable facts about the Chinese is that, whereas all the other supremely distinguished peoples through the historical millenia, such as the Egyptians, the Persians, the Greeks, the Romans and for that matter the British, have each in turn risen to splendid greatness during one considerable period and then declined to comparative unimportance never to rise again to pre-eminent influence, the Chinese have achieved

Ladies of the court, Tang period painting

a succession of such ups and downs through several thousand years. Each rise was followed by a fall, and each fall was in due course followed by another rise to eminence. I must not speculate here on the reason for that, and shall merely repeat that one of those resurrections is now once more occurring.

At the beginning of the twentieth century the Chinese nation was extremely weak. Ruled by the once upon a time noble but by then degenerate Qing (Ch'ing) Dynasty, it was badly stuck in ruts of an antiquated, seriously out-of-date past. This was partly because until a few decades earlier the Emperors and their mandarin officials had kept their people more or less isolated from the rest of humanity. They regarded their Imperial realm – which they believed to be the Central Kingdom bestowed on them by the Mandate of Heaven – as the only civilized state on Earth, and viewed the rest of mankind as "barbarians" who could be treated with contempt. During much of

A flower seller carrying on business in war torn Shanghai, 1938

the previous two and a half centuries a succession of Qing Emperors had indeed presided over one of the fine eras of Chinese civilization in the artistic and other cultural fields; but in economic affairs their Oriental domain had slipped far behind certain Occidental kingdoms. Mostly as a result of the Industrial Revolution, some European nations were developing very strongly their economic power, and as a consequence they were extending their political influence into wider parts of the world. The Spanish, Dutch, British, French and other overseas empires were growing mightily.

By the mid-nineteenth century the British and certain others wished to expand their profitable commercial trading into China as well as other regions of Asia and, as a consequence of Chinese resistance to this, military conflicts broke out. In the Opium War and similar contests the Westerners' much more modernly equipped naval ships

Opposite : The tomb of Sun Yat Sen, Nanjing

Left : An opium smoker in Shanghai, 1938

and regiments of soldiers inflicted defeats on the rather primitively armed Chinese boats and troops. As a result the victors imposed on the Qing rulers humiliating peace terms which became known as "the Unequal Treaties".

At the opening of the twentieth century China's old-fashioned national economy still remained almost entirely confined to extremely simple agricultural production and cottage industry outputs. The comparatively few modern mills and factories which existed in some cities were owned and managed by foreigners, including in some cases Japanese. In nearby Japan the up-and-coming native people had succeeded remarkably well through the last thirty years in leaping in economic affairs out of the Middle Ages into the twentieth century. But China continued to be in every way an antique feudalistic society. Its Imperial, aristocratic and other élite families were very rich, and almost the whole of the rest of the population were extremely poor. Nearly all its multitudinous peasants, who composed an overwhelming majority of the populace, were serfs – and indeed virtual slaves – of their landlords or other masters. The influence exerted by the wealthy landed gentry on government policies was very great since most of the bureaucrats sprang from their families.

This state of affairs had begun to provoke rebellious thoughts in the minds of some of the Chinese intellectuals, especially those who had been for a while students in universities in Western lands. They believed that radical political, social and economic reforms based on French, British and American practices should be introduced into China, so that the Chinese people could enjoy a freer and more prosperously modern way of life. As a result of agitation which they initiated, a revolution erupted in southern China in 1911.

Two very contrasting groups of Chinese contrived in collaboration together the auspicious events which occurred through the next year. The more significant of them was the party of mostly youthful Chinese some of whom had resided overseas, and who wished their nation's government to be reformed in ways modelled on those existing in the Western democracies. Under Sun Yat-sen's leadership they started the rebellion which gained a lot of support in southern China, where the Qing Dynasty had for long been rather unpopular. Sun Yat-sen became the President of a Republican regime which they established in Guangzhou (Canton). Afterwards armed forces that they mobilized advanced successfully into central China. But the revolt was not so acceptable further north, and the Emperor's army halted their progress in the Yangtse River valley. Then the Commander-in-Chief of that army, General Yuan Shikai (Yuan Shih-kai), betrayed the Imperial cause and negotiated an agreement with Sun Yat-sen by which he and his troops supported the establishment of a nation-wide republic – on one condition. The condition was that Yuan Shikai himself should be its first president. Recognizing the difficulty of achieving further military gains, wishing the republic to be extended throughout the country, and trusting Yuan's word, Sun and his colleagues accepted this arrangement.

As a consequence the reigning Emperor was forced to abdicate from the throne in 1912. The monarchy was abolished, and a republic was established in its place.

The general was in fact not a sincere republican. On the contrary, an old-fashioned monarchist who had grown disenchanted with the Qings, he nursed a private ambition to end their rule and – as had happened periodically throughout earlier Chinese history – replace it by a new Royal Dynasty of which he would be the founder-

Emperor. He therefore secretly regarded the creation of the republic as a temporary expedient which would be succeeded before long by a restoration of the monarchy under his own personal Imperial rule.

Three years later he appeared to be on the verge of achieving that aim when another development thwarted it. Through the last two decades the increasingly powerful Japanese had been gradually extending their suzerainty over certain territories which previously were parts of the Chinese Empire, such as Korea, Manchuria and Formosa Island. The militarist governors in Tokyo desired their now quite strongly modernised nation to become the overlord of the whole of the Far East, including still weak, unmodernised China. In 1915 they presented Yuan Shikai's government in Beijing (Peking) with their notorious Twenty-one Demands, which, if accepted, would in effect have accomplished that ambitious plan.

Yuan's somewhat compromising response angered Sun Yat-sen and his adherents. At the same time it gave some of Yuan's fellow generals, who felt jealous of his growing authority, an opportunity to declare opposition to him. They took strong action against him, and he fell from power. Then those generals became rivals of one another, in some cases helped to do so by financial support from the Japanese. Commanding separate groups of armed forces, they fought against each other for control of this or that region of the vast country.

Sun Yat-sen and his colleagues were forced to withdraw again to the south, where they re-established their administration in Guangzhou.

The warlords period of chaotic disunity in China began.

2 The Warlords Interlude

SUN YAT-SEN AND HIS COLLEAGUES WERE UNTRAINED AND INEXPERIENCED IN GOVERNMENT. Moreover, the popularly elected parliament which they established in Guangzhou was, contrary to their passionately sincere wishes, corrupt as well as inefficient. This was of course all partly because that democratic institution was a completely alien form of rule in China, with no roots in the native political soil. Through a myriad centuries the Chinese people had been accustomed to wholly autocratic government in which neither they themselves nor their chosen representatives played any part.

Nor did the Guangzhou regime command a strong professional army of its own which could check this or that general's battalions from asserting his power in other parts of south as well as north, east, west and central China. And the continuing rivalries of those warlords made them unwilling to combine their military forces in support of one government of a united China. To make matters worse, their often ill-disciplined soldiers ravaged the countrysides, causing the landed gentry to withdraw for safety into the cities and subjecting the masses of peasants to even harsher oppression and poverty. In the urban areas, too, except for a comparatively small number of rich military and civilian individuals and families, almost all the people were miserably poor.

For these various reasons the government in Guangzhou failed to implement the policies of economic, social and other reforms in the nation's internal affairs which they advocated, and which could have gained them helpful popular support by starting to improve the ordinary people's living conditions. In external affairs also their aims were frustrated. Sun Yat-sen tried to secure recognition of his regime by the Western powers as the legitimate government of China; but partly because of the confused internal situation throughout the land, and partly because of those powers' involvement by then as belligerents in the first World War (with Japan as one of their allies) they rejected his plea. Instead they retained their Diplomatic Missions in the old capital of Beijing (then of course still called Peking) where they maintained official relations with whatever warlord's administration happened to rule there at the moment.

Those were the days when Western Imperialism flourished in much of Asia and other parts of the world. The British, French, Dutch or some other European power ruled over India, Ceylon, the Netherlands East Indies and numerous other Oriental lands. Some of these, such as French Indo-China, Portuguese Macao and British Hong Kong and Burma, were territories which in fairly recent times had been parts of China's extensive realm.

China itself was not a colony of any foreign nation; yet in certain ways important areas of it were subject to alien rule. The "Unequal Treaties" imposed on its earlier Emperors in the mid-nineteenth century had established that certain municipal regions in Shanghai, Nanking (now Nanjing), Canton (now Guangzhou), and several other cities were governed, policed and in other ways administered as so-called "Concessions" by the small minorities of local British, French, German, Japanese and/or other non-Chinese residents. These were the districts where modern industrial enterprises were developed, almost all of which were owned and managed by foreigners. And their products were protected against competition from elsewhere inside or outside China by arrangements which prevented the Chinese government from introducing duties or taxes at rates which might hurt them. To ensure that this protection was effective foreign officials were in charge of the nation's Customs Administration. In addition all the alien inhabitants throughout the country enjoyed "extraterritorial rights" by which they were free from trials in Chinese courts according to Chinese law and could be plaintiffs or defendants only in local foreign-managed courts where the law of their own native land mostly prevailed. Some overseas governments exercised other privileges also, such as the ability to send their naval gunboats into China's territorial waters and up its rivers.

Sun Yat-sen's government were earnest Nationalists who wished to bring this state of affairs to an end, and to restore complete sovereignty to the Chinese people as a fully independent nation. They sought to start negotiations with the Western governments about the problem; but those governments refused to enter into any such discussions.

Then an event occurred which initiated a notable development in China's external relations and in its people's internal outlooks. In 1917 the Tsarist regime in Russia had been overthrown, and soon afterwards Lenin's Communist government came to power there. Hitherto the Russians had not only acquired considerable territories alongside Siberia which they seized by conquest from earlier Chinese suzerainty, but also shared all the extraterritorial rights and other privileges enjoyed by foreigners inside China. In 1920 the authorities in Moscow voluntarily relinquished these rights and privileges; and in the following year they sent an envoy to Shanghai for talks with Sun Yat-sen. As a result of their discussions the Soviet government established Diplomatic relations with Sun's government in Guangzhou, appointed Russian advisers to assist it there, and gave it other useful aid. Moreover, although a joint statement issued after the Shanghai

Opposite : Part of the Great Wall, near the Nanjing Gate. Built in the 4th and 3rd centuries BC it is almost 4,000 miles long ; the only man-made building visible from the moon

talks expressed the view that Communism was not suited to China, Sun Yat-sen agreed that the recently formed Chinese Communist Party should be a working ally with his own Nationalist (now known in Chinese terminology as the Kuomintang) Party in all its endeavours. Individual Communists could join the latter as full members. And soon afterwards the Kuomintang organization was reshaped somewhat on the lines of the Soviet's Communist Party, with political commissars, strictly autocratic discipline, and a mass propaganda organization. Its leaders declared that their ultimate aim continued to be the creation of a parliamentary democracy in China, but that a period of tutelage would first be required during which, under authoritarian guidance, the people could acquire the necessary experience and skills to govern themselves. How long that period of tutelage was intended to last was anybody's guess.

In 1925 Sun Yat-sen died during a visit to Beijing, where he had tried, unsuccessfully, to persuade the current local warlord – the "Christian General" Feng Yuxiang (Feng Yu-hsiang) – to help to re-establish a united China by co-operating with the government in Guangzhou.

After his death the Kuomintang leaders dropped any plans for radical or social reforms inside China as one of their primary objectives. They gave first priority to the patriotic causes of overthrowing the divisive rule by warlords, abolishing by negotiations with overseas governments the foreign concessions in various cities, withdrawing the extraterritorial rights and other privileges enjoyed by alien residents, and so restoring China's complete unity and independence as a sovereign state.

An event which occurred in the International Settlement in Shanghai on May 30th, 1925 gained them widespread popular support for these aims. A crowd of Chinese students demonstrating there against the arrests of Chinese workers on strike in a Japanese cotton mill was fired upon by police commanded by foreign officers, and some of the youngsters were killed. Neither the warlord who controlled the Shanghai region nor any other of those military tyrants made firm protests against this. The Kuomintang government, on the other hand, denounced it furiously as "Imperialist oppression", and a passionate response flared-up among people throughout the land. They expressed their emotional anti-foreign sentiment by organizing a successful boycott of British and Japanese goods, which extended also into near-by Hong Kong. In public propaganda the warlords were condemned as "running dogs of the Imperialists".

Early in 1926 the Kuomintang army, commanded by General Chiang Kai-shek, started to march north from Guangzhou to reconquer the various provinces governed by one or another of those despots. It advanced quite quickly, and by the summer had captured Hankou (Hankow), Wuchang (Wu Chang) and Hanyang (Han Yang) in the Yangste River valley. Before the year's end it had also occupied Nanjing, and early in 1927 was closing in on Shanghai. Then a portentous event occurred in that city.

Through the previous few years the alliance between the Kuomintang and the Communist Parties had worked in an ill-defined way. The latter group's leaders were not interested simply in the regaining of national unity and freedom from external intrusions; they were equally fervently dedicated to achieving an internal social revolution which would liberate the masses of poor Chinese from oppression by their landlords and other masters. Whilst the Kuomintang chiefs concentrated their efforts on the first of those causes, the Communist zealots therefore concentrated theirs on the second. They penetrated rural and urban areas where multitudes of poverty-stricken

Above : Samples of arms carried on the Long March, Shaoshan Museum

Below : An austere dormitory in the Peasants Memorial Institute, Guangzhou. Here, in 1926, Mao worked with Zhou Enlai and others who were to become leaders of the revolution

Above : A painting in the Shaoshan Museum showing the dispossession of the Landlords after the revolution

Opposite : Statue of Chairman Mao at Nanjing Bridge

Below : Painting of Chairman Mao leading the Long March. It began on March 16, 1934 ending 370 days later when the 20,000 survivors, a quarter of the original force, reached Shaanxi, a journey of 6,000 miles

people lived, and conducted socialist propaganda campaigns inciting them against their oppressors.

After the impassioned popular reaction to the May 30th incident in Shanghai the British government had sent a battalion of troops to garrison the International Settlement there, and in addition had despatched British gunboats up the Yangtse River to anchor off Nanjing and Hankou, where foreign Concessions also existed. These moves increased the emotional resentment of the local populace, and when Kuomintang troops captured first Hankou and afterwards Nanjing violent actions, including some killings, were committed against the foreign residents. Then, as Chiang Kai-shek's regiments approached Shanghai, the workers in the Chinese-governed district of that city rose under Communist instigation and wrested control of it from the local warlord. A few days later Chiang and his soldiers arrived there. He felt deeply angered by that prior Communist "coup", and a confrontation between him and those alleged allies promptly occurred. At his orders their militia were disarmed, their political leaders who failed to slip away swiftly to safety were arrested, and those individuals were executed.

In the meantime the Kuomintang civilian government had moved from Guangzhon to Wuhan (Wu Han) in the wake of its army's advance. Its membership there was dominated by somewhat left-wing politicians, and Chiang ignored it. Instead he set up his own more right-wing administration in Nanjing. For a while the Wuhan group wavered, but soon most of its individuals decided to support his regime. The breach between the Kuomintang and the Communist parties became complete. The Russian advisers to the Kuomintang were sent home to Moscow, and the Chinese Communist leaders and their supporters retreated into a mountainous region in Hunan Province.

In 1928 Chiang's army resumed its advance north. Achieving one military success after another, it eventually drove the last powerful warlord from Beijing. He was the renowned Manchuian General Zhang Zuolin (Chang Tso-lin), who hastily got into a train to escape to his hereditary seat of rule, Shenyang (Mukden).

The warlords' interlude in modern Chinese history drew to a close.

3 Kuomintang China

GENERALISSIMO (AS HE NOW BECAME KNOWN) CHIANG KAI-SHEK WAS FIRMLY INSTALLED as the political as well as the military head of the Kuomintang government. He and his colleagues transferred the capital from Beijing to Nanjing, where the Western and other foreign nations, including Russia, recognized his regime as the legitimate government of a now more or less reunited China.

A year later, towards the end of 1929, I happened to make my first visit to China. During it I met a partial survival of the warlord period, for in Shenyang I held talks with young General Zhang Xueliang (Chang Hsueh-liang) who ruled Manchuria. He was the son of General Zhang Zuolin, the formidable military tyrant who had first governed that province, then expanded his sway to cover the rest of north-east China by driving General Feng Yuxiang from Beijing, then himself been expelled from his overlordship there by Chiang Kai-shek's army, and finally been killed on his retreat back to Shenyang in a railway accident contrived by the Japanese, who did not want him to return as the mighty self-assertive Ruler of Manchuria. They were by then contemplating bringing that materially rather wealthy domain completely under their own iron rule.

Zhang Xueliang was by nature a wise as well as pleasant young man. He wished his fellow Manchurians to be free from that foreign control, and to remain citizens of an autonomous territory closely associated with China, owing loyalty to the Kuomintang government in Nanjing. He told me of his fear of possible Japanese aggression.

On further travels during my stay in the country I caught ghost-like glimpses of an even earlier period of its history – the fabulous Old Cathay which in the Revolution of 1911–12 had been banished from the scene. This was not simply when I viewed magnificent historical monuments like the Great Wall of China, the Ming Tombs, the Forbidden City in Beijing and the gracious Temple of Heaven near-by. One

Above : Tomb painting in Shaanxi of a camel convoy startled by polo players

Opposite top : A buffalo drawing a wooden harrow in the Hangzhou rice fields

Opposite bottom : a worker with his bamboo carrying pole, a method in use for over 2,000 years

day as I rode on a Mongolian pony across the plain to the Western Hills I dropped in for a while at a farmhouse where some still alive but no longer kicking survivors of the dead past dwelt in their retirement. They were a group of aged eunuchs who had been high and rather mighty court flunkeys in the Imperial Palace during the rule of the famous (or should I write infamous?) Empress Dowager Tz'u Hsi. They spoke nostalgically about those "good old days"; and as they described in high-pitched voices their semi-regal way of life then their portly figures, pig-tailed hair and mandarin-style costumes almost brought to life again in my imagination that deceased era.

Other survivors of the past ambled across the plain that day. Occasionally as I trotted on my steed a caravan of camels processed past me carrying aloft on their humped backs loads of merchandise which they had brought from beyond the Gobi Desert for sale in China's old capital – exactly as countless generations of their forebears had done along the renowned Silk Road through thousands of years. Sauntering sedately by, they were a picturesque vision of a piece of antique history. They themselves seemed to think that history had not changed at all, for they glanced at me haughtily down their snooty long noses as if I were a "barbarian" from some uncivilized overseas land.

24

But history was in fact still very much on the move inside as well as outside China. The monarchy had now been firmly replaced by a republic, and although the nation remained in some ways archaically weak it was starting to show signs of becoming more modernly strong. Capable Chinese, for example, were successfully establishing their own industrial and commercial businesses. The Western powers which through most of a century had treated China with disrepsect were beginning to revise that attitude. They felt some regard for the Kuomintang regime which had defeated the warlords and re-created a more united country. Indeed, the British and some other governments expressed a readiness to consider starting negotiations with the Nanjing authorities about a possible revision of the "Unequal Treaties" which could progressively over a period of years restore the Chinese nation's complete sovereign independence.

In a small way I was involved in discussions concerning that prospect. I had gone to the Far East as a secretary to the British delegation attending an international conference held in Japan's lovely pristine capital, Kyoto. The gathering consisted of groups of eminent and influential, although non-governmental, representatives of the United States of America, Canada, Australia, New Zealand, Japan and China as well as Britain. They discussed the major international problems then affecting relations between the governments exercising responsibilities in lands surrounding the Pacific Ocean, including the need for alterations in the treaties with China. After the conference ended I went for some travels in China, and during my stay there two or three of the important British delegates from the conference also arrived. We held semi-official talks with Kuomintang authorities and other personalities about possible first moves towards a gradual ending of the British residents' extraterritorial rights, the foreign rule of the International Settlement in Shanghai, and the British Concessions in various other cities.

My father happened to be Britain's Prime Minister then, so many doors were wide open to welcome me in Nanjing and elsewhere. Chiang Kai-shek himself was engaged on some military operations away from the capital, but among those whom I met were his charming and influential wife Mei-ling, her very able brother T. V. Soong who was the Minister of Finance, and several other Ministers including Sun Yat-sen's son Sun Fo. I had serious discussions with them all about the current situation in China and the relations between our two countries.

To anticipate for a moment, although the British government did quickly make some minor preliminary reductions in the privileges enjoyed by their citizens in China, and did give up the British Concessions in a few of the less important cities (whilst retaining them in all the more important ones), the official negotiations on the major questions dragged on through the next few years, and had not yet been concluded when (as I shall describe later) an all-out Japanese invasion drove Chiang Kai-shek's government out of Nanjing and most of the rest of the country.

As I have already mentioned, he and his colleagues showed no interest in introducing economic and social reforms which would improve the lot of the masses of their compatriots, who then numbered about 400,000,000 people. Throughout the vast rural areas, for instance, an overwhelming majority of the multitudes of peasants continued to be poverty-stricken. They were often so half-starved that in order to be able to buy enough food to keep themselves alive parents had to sell their children to their landlords or other tycoons, and frequently husbands were for the same reason forced to sell their wives.

A peasant watering his crops, Shanghai, 1938

During my stay in Beijing in 1929 I observed a sad example of those tragic break-ups of family life, which continued to occur exactly as they had done through centuries. I was a guest of the British Minister, Sir Miles Lampson, in his delightful old mandarin's mansion there. One evening I was embarrassed to learn that he had assumed that I – a bachelor in my late twenties – would wish one of my experiences in China to be jumping into bed with a "sing-song girl", as prostitutes there were called. He had therefore arranged for one of his Legation officers who could speak the local language to guide me to a brothel in the "red light" district, introduce me to some seductive young female, and then go and have drinks with friends near-by whilst I was otherwise engaged. The fellow would return at an appointed hour to lead me home again.

I had no desire for any such experience. However, I was too shy to say "No", and in any case I thought it could be interesting to meet the damsel, ask my guide to explain that she need not undress, and to add that I would like to sit for a while chatting with her about life in China. The youthful civil servant probably thought that I had gone mad; but he agreed to stay and play his part as the interpreter in the odd scene.

Overleaf: Buffalo file across a causeway at Guilin at sunset

The beautiful little Chinese whore was astonished at my abstemious suggestion, and smiled bashfully but friendly as we sat down to talk. Her tiny room had no furniture except a double bed and a single chair, the latter object presumably being provided simply to accommodate a man's discarded jacket, trousers and underwear whilst the pair embraced each other naked on the couch. My interpreter occupied the chair instead, whilst she and I sat upright instead of lying flat, and fully clad, instead of nude on the bed.

For two hours we gossiped relaxedly and very pleasantly. I learned that she was a youngster still in her middle teens whose parents had been poor peasants. Her happiest, most cherished memories concerned her infant years with them, in spite of their impoverished family existence. Alas! she had not seen or heard of them for many years, and did not even know whether they were still alive. She had been sold twice – first as a child by her helpless father to their landlord, and later by that alleged gentleman to a pimp. Hence her present occupation.

The generally very poor living conditions of much of the population was evident in cities where Foreign Concessions existed. In Tianjin (Tientsin), for example, I visited both the British Concession and the Chinese administered municipal area alongside it. The difference between the two was almost incredible. When one stepped from one to the other the broad, smooth surfaced, clean streets in the former suddenly turned into narrow, bumpy, pot-holed and dirty lanes in the latter. Indeed, one day I went along a street the middle of which was the boundary between the two burghs. The British half of the roadway was in excellent hard-surfaced repair, whilst the other half was in an appalling state of muddy disrepair. Again, the buildings in the former were quite handsome and the housing for the Chinese workers was neat and comfortable, whereas the appearance of the latter was slum-like. I should add the comment that it looked even worse than the still extremely awful areas of Limehouse in the East End of London, England at that time, which I knew because I represented that constituency then on the London County Council.

The Kuomintang leaders' unconcern about any improvement in the living conditions of the humble people was by then the principal difference between their outlook and that of their earlier allies, the Communists. When Chiang Kai-shek declared his enmity towards the Reds following the Shanghai episode they withdrew to a mountainous area in Jiangxi (Kiangsi) where they hoped to be able to mobilize some armed forces, continue their political propaganda activities among the peasantry, and form a strong base from which they could later advance towards attaining the dominant influence in the government of changing China. Under the great revolutionary leader Mao Zedong (Mao Tse-tung) they began to work towards that destiny. He was supported by a team of enthusiastic comrades, the most able among whom were the politician Zhou Enlai (Chou En-lai) and the soldier General Zhu De (Chu Teh). The former had been the principal organizer of the Communist "coup" in Shanghai in 1927, and had fortunately managed to escape when Chiang Kai-shek ordered the arrests and executions of its chiefs. The latter had been the commanding officer of a Kuomintang army unit which mutinied against Chiang's regime later in 1927 and switched its support to the Communists. Each one of that trinity of rebel geniuses was still a young man, but their splendid, diverse and complementary qualities as leaders of men were

Barbed wire being wheeled to the war zone, Shanghai, 1938. The Chinese invented the wheelbarrow to negotiate the narrow paths between the fields

already ripe. A military as well as political conflict between the Kuomintang and the Communists began.

Through the next twenty years the rivalry between them was to be the most significant development in Chinese affairs.

During much of that period the new division of loyalties which it caused among the Chinese people gave the Japanese an opportunity to pursue their ambition to extend their Imperial rule over large areas, and they hoped in due time the whole, of the country. To begin with they annexed Manchuria outright, compelling Zhang Xueliang and his army to withdraw further south. They installed the young, abdicated ex-Emperor Pu Yi as it is crowned head and their obedient puppet. Then they invaded and secured control of Chengde (Jehol) Province, and later virtually detached much of north China from effective administration by the government in Nanjing. Stationing ever larger Japanese military forces in cities like Tianjin, Quingdao (Tsing Tao) and Shanghai, they used those centres as bases for further infiltrations or assaults. Eventually, in the late mid-1930s – when the Western nations were preoccupied with the critical events threatening to erupt into a second World War – they launched an all-out invasion for the conquest of the whole of China.

In spite of the Kuomintang government's declared dedication to the cause of National Independence, during the first several years of these developments they failed to take any effective action against the foreign aggressor. On the contrary, they deployed their army to fight instead against their Communist fellow-countrymen further south, denouncing them as "rebels and bandits". Proclaiming that their aim was "internal

Young Red Guards in front of their Desert Farm Commune near Beijing

pacification before resistance to external attack", they no doubt sincerely expected that their much larger and better equipped battalions would quickly exterminate the Communist dissidents, and that they would then be able from a reliably firm base to mobilize their whole military forces against the Japanese foe. However, that expectation never got realized. Between 1931 and 1934 they launched a succession of offensive campaigns to inflict defeat on the comparatively small rebel troops in and around their mountainous retreats in Jiangxi; but one after another these all failed. This was partly because the insurgents developed increasing skills in the conduct of guerrilla warfare, and partly because the policy of land reform which Mao and his comrades were implementing in every area which they controlled gained them very helpful support from the local peasantry.

After four years of military frustrations Chiang Kai-shek adopted a different method for exterminating them. He organized his army and other encircling forces to impose an economic blockade on the Reds in their highland resorts. When this threatened to prove successful Mao and his host of political and military adherents managed to break through the Kuomintang's lines by a secret route, and started on their famous Long March. Through the next almost two years they continued trudging onward for thousands of miles, often in extremely difficult circumstances in harsh country, until they arrived in the remote north-western province of Shaanxi (Shensi). There they established their new headquarters.

As I have indicated, in addition to their growing ability as guerrilla warriors an important reason for their success was the active support which their radical social and economic policies gained for them from the local grassroots population wherever they settled. They confiscated the land from the landlords, distributed it among the peasants as its new owners, and in other ways also relieved those rustics from earlier hardships, such as exploitation by usurers. And whereas the Kuomintang troops, like those of the warlords, treated the rural masses with contempt as inferiors, billeting themselves upon them for no rent, stealing their food, raping their wives and daughters, and often killing villagers, the Red Army soldiers treated the local inhabitants everywhere with complete respect. They paid for their food and lodgings, helped them in various ways in their agricultural labours, and showed an entirely decent friendliness towards females and males alike – genial conduct which those humble folk had never experienced before from armed soldiery. It won their hearts.

In the much vaster areas of the country under Kuomintang control the government introduced no such land reform or other benevolent social changes, although these had been foreshadowed by Sun Yat-sen. Nor did its Ministers give any indication as to when the autocratic "period of tutelage" prior to the introduction of political democracy might end. Indeed, their actions suggested that it would probably never end. The Generalissimo and his group of personal adherents kept rejecting proposals for the enactment of a constitution which would establish an elected legislative assembly, and took unto themselves more and more dictatorial power. The latter attitude did not worry the ordinary people at all, but it began to alienate many of the liberal-minded intellectuals who had previously supported Sun Yat-sen's Kuomintang.

Another development caused other members of the upper classes as well to consider perhaps switching their sympathies to the Communists. Zealous Nationalists, those educated citizens felt increasingly critical of Chiang's failure to resist the Japanese aggressors. Mao Zedong and his comrades sincerely shared that sentiment; and they exploited it. Some time before they set out from Jiangxi on the Long March they had published a declaration of war against the Japanese. This was then a purely nominal act of hostility, because in their small areas of occupation in southern China they could not make any military strikes against the foreign enemy invading the north. But that situation changed after they arrived in Shaanxi. Indeed, one of the reasons why they plodded so far into the distant north-west may well have been that there they would be in a geographical position to hit at the Japanese. And after their arrival they repeated their declaration of war against those aggressors, appealed for a cessation of the civil war between themselves and the Kuomintang, and declared themselves ready to co-operate amicably with Chiang's forces against the foreign foe.

In another way, too, they were now wooing their bourgeois compatriots. Whereas in the south they had treated the landlords and other earlier oppressors of the peasantry very badly, often not simply confiscating their property but also causing them to be killed, after their arrival in the north they adopted a partially different attitude. They still deprived those landed gentry of their estates and other privileges, but otherwise treated them fairly as equal members in an egalitarian society. They emphasized their desire that the whole Chinese people should unite to expel the Japanese from their homeland, and spread around the slogan "Chinese do not fight Chinese".

The Kuomintang leaders were not impressed. They regarded the Communists as dangerous rivals to their government whose revolutionary policies would destroy the conservative Chinese society which they favoured. Towards the end of 1936 Chiang Kai-shek therefore planned another military offensive against them, on a scale which he reckoned would really destroy them.

Opposite : William MacQuitty's house in the French Concession, Shanghai 1938. Ali Baba, a Saluki, plays in the foreground

Above : the houses of the Chinese poor contrasted with the tall new buildings in Shanghai. A boy plays the old Chinese game of Diabolo, wearing clothing heavily padded against the severe winter of 1938

However, the principal units of his army in the north which he ordered to conduct the attack felt averse to the proposal. They were the Manchurian troops commanded by General Zhang Xueliang who had earlier been forced to withdraw from their native region, and who deeply resented the virtually unopposed occupation of it by the Japanese. They wished to recapture it, and so felt sympathy with the Communists' plea for an end of the civil war and the start of a united national war to drive out the foreign invaders.

To ensure that in the circumstances his orders were carried out, Generalissimo Chiang Kai-shek himself went to Xian (Sian) in Shaanxi. The result of his visit was the very opposite. In a not unfriendly but nonetheless resolute mood Zhang Xueliang had him in effect arrested, and initiated negotiations between him and the Communists. With the help of Mao Zedong's persuasive envoy Zhou Enlai, he induced Chiang to accept their policy of re-establishing a working alliance between the Kuomintang and the Communists for the attainment of their joint patriotic nationalist purpose. In return for his acceptance of it the Communists agreed that he should remain the Head of

State and be the Commander-in-Chief of their combined military forces. This was a nominal more than a practical arrangement but, it "saved his face". Thus internal pacification was achieved, and co-operative resistance to external attack began.

I need not take space here to recount the details of the consequent struggle against the Japanese. For a while the Kuomintang army put up quite a good resistance against them, but later the resistance collapsed. At the end of 1937 the enemy captured their capital Nanjing, and Chiang and his Ministers retreated to Hankou. In the latter part of 1938 the Japanese captured Hankou, and soon afterwards Guangzhou also fell to them. The Kuomintang leaders were forced to withdraw their government to Chongqing (Chungking) in the far distant western hills. There its army engaged in virtually nothing but defensive operations, making no serious attacks against the foe. By the end of 1939, when the World War had broken out in Europe, the Japanese occupation appeared to cover about three-quarters of the whole of China.

Their effective administration was, however, much more limited, being largely confined to the cities, main towns and principal routes of communications between them. Mao's now very numerous, but each comparatively small and therefore swiftly mobile, units of guerrilla fighters controlled considerable areas of the countrysides, where the Communist civil administrators were very friendly and helpful to the rural population. For geographical as well as other reasons their command and activities were now independent of control by the government in remote Chongqing. This state of affairs persisted through the next few years, because after the Japanese entered the wider war as allies of Nazi Germany in 1941 their military forces became preoccupied with the conquests of various territories in South East Asia. So the stalemate in China remained. It continued until the explosions of atomic bombs in Hiroshima and Nagasaki compelled the Japanese to surrender to the Western powers.

Those powers still maintained diplomatic relations with the Kuomintang government in Chongqing. In the meantime mutual suspicions and even enmity had been resurging between it and its Communist allies. The success of Mao's guerrilla fighters in limiting Japanese rule through much of the country of supposed enemy occupation had gained them increasing regard among not only masses of the ordinary people but also growing numbers of members of the educated classes. The Kuomintang leaders resented this, and their wish to suppress the Communists revived. When the Japanese withdrew from the country all the cities that they had held were surrendered to Chiang Kai-shek's regime as the legal government of China, and a resumption of the earlier civil war between the two Chinese parties threatened.

In an attempt to prevent this the sagacious American General Marshall was sent to China to endeavour to persuade the two to co-operate as partners together governing a peacefully re-united China. But his efforts failed. The two sides were in fact now irreconcilable. The Communists were determined to achieve their revolutionary aims, whilst the Kuomintang leaders resolutely maintained their reactionary outlook. Violent warfare broke out once more between them.

In the renewed struggle the Americans gave considerable military and other aid to Chiang Kai-shek's government because of the passionate anti-Communist beliefs of

Chinese children are fascinated by a foreigner and hope for a share of his purchase, others watch a noodle-seller. As Passports were unnecessary thousands of European refugees found shelter in Shanghai

the authorities in Washington; and the other Western nations continued to give it their diplomatic recognition. But that foreign assistance was an inadequate substitute for the support of the multitudinous Chinese people. By then not only masses of the peasants but also countless radical-minded members of the middle and even upper classes had become disenchanted with Chiang Kai-shek and his clique, not only because of their failure to take effective action against the Japanese but also because of their current conservative policies in internal affairs in contradiction to the changes foreshadowed by Sun Yat-sen. In particular many educated members of the young generation transferred their sympathies to the Communists, and went to areas controlled by them to give them active help. Inside the Kuomintang Party itself a liberal-inclined group of members became critical of Chiang's administration; but they were unable to oust him and his inner circle of colleagues from power.

The conflict dragged on for almost three more years. During it the Red Army's soldiers became well trained in conventional as well as guerrilla warfare, and they inflicted a succession of defeats on their opponents. By the end of 1948 they were on the point of completing their occupation of Manchuria and the whole of northern

The Shanghai Hunt carried on regardless of war, but to the anger of the tidy vegetable farmers who threw ordure at any who came near. The hunt secretary later paid compensation for any damage that had been done

China, where Kuomintang troops still held out in only a few cities, including Beijing. Communist military forces had also over-run much of central China and were advancing along the north shore of the Yangtse River. They threatened to attack Nanjing on its southern shore, where the now demoralized Kuomintang government lingered.

At that critical moment, late in 1948, I revisited China. I had recently become Britain's Commissioner General in South East Asia, a sort of roving Ambassador with responsibilities for co-ordinating our political, diplomatic and other policies regarding the five British colonial territories and the half-dozen foreign ruled countries in that region, with in addition some duties concerning Hong Kong. The potential developments in near-by China could affect very significantly the South East Asian prospect, and I wished to observe the situation there at close quarters, learning about it in discussions with some of my eminent Chinese acquaintances as well as our British Ambassador in Nanjing. I talked with Chiang Kai-shek and his wife, and with the Foreign Minister George Yeh, the Minister for Trade and Commerce H. H. Kung, and other important persons there. Afterwards I went to Shanghai, and then stayed for a few days with T. V. Soong in Guangzhou. The Generalissimo had appointed him as the Governor of Southern China, presumably in the hope that his outstanding abilities would organize all the region's resources in ways which made it an unconquerable political and military fortress where the Kuomintang could, if necessary, make not simply a last-ditch stand but a strong resistance which would turn the tide of war and start their reconquest of the rest of China.

In Nanjing I got a clear impression that many of the authorities feared this might be indulgence in wishful thinking, and that they were privately preparing to pack their bags for a retreat from China's mainland shores to Formosa Island.

That was in fact what quite soon happened. Very early in 1949 the Kuomintang armed defenders of Beijing surrendered, and Mao Zedong established his government in that ancient capital. Through the next several months the Red Army steadily gained control of the whole of mainland China. In the autumn Chiang Kai-shek and his colleagues did sail across the sea to Formosa, where they set up their Kuomintang regime.

During their twenty-two years of somewhat hit-and-miss rule Chiang and his Nationalist team had achieved some good things for China. One was the overthrow of the warlords who had fragmented and despoiled the country through a dozen earlier years. They also began to plan and implement some long overdue modern developments in certain of the vast country's very out-of-date economic and related affairs, such as the building of road and rail communications between its hitherto considerably unconnected north and south, east and west – although many of these projects had scarcely proceeded beyond the drawing-boards by 1949. In addition they had begun to win more respect for the Chinese nation in the outside world than had existed for a century. Indeed, after the end of the World War, Britain and the European powers yielded up the foreign Concessions in various cities to Chinese administration, and they also renounced all the extraterritorial rights and other privileges previously retained by aliens in China.

However, the Kuomintang rulers' policies brought no benefits to the masses of their fellow countrymen. On the contrary, the poverty of a vast majority of the people throughout the urban and rural areas which they controlled continued to be appalling.

I saw a lot of it during my second visit there; one could not help glimpsing it almost wherever one looked. In the cities many beggars loitered in every street. Most of the people were extremely poor, living in hovels, having no security of work or pay, and often being seriously under-nourished. Child labour was common, boys and girls being recruited for work at 8 or 9 years old for no wages beyond inadequate food dished out to them – often just one bowl of rice each day.

In the rural regions which the Kuomintang controlled, where an overwhelming majority of the population lived, statistics record that 10% of the people were landlords or "rich" peasants, 20% were "middle" peasants who owned a little land and lived quite comfortably, but 70% were "poor" peasants. The members of the first group were often decoratively dressed, and those of the second wore quite pleasant clothes, but most of the third were a very sad sight. They usually possessed nothing except the ragged garments in which they stood up, plus perhaps a small tin pot for cooking rice a wood fire on the floor of the often windowless single-room shack in which they were lodged. Frequently they were in debt to usurers, and parents were still often so poverty-stricken that they had to sell their children as slaves to landlords. Sometimes husbands had no choice but to sell their wives as well. A typical case of this was the father of three youngsters who had been compelled to sell his wife and two of the children. A while later when it appeared that he must sell his only remaining

In 1938 the Japanese gave the Federal Reserve Bank of North China the sole right of note issue, a ruse intended to give them currency to raid the foreign exchange reserves of the Chinese Government which responded by devaluing the national dollar from 1s. 2d. to 8d. The Chinese printer of the new notes showed Confucius making what appears to be a rude gesture with his fingers.

son, he could not bring himself to do so, and committed suicide instead. The boy stayed alive as a homeless waif – until the Revolution of 1949 brought him a new prospect of life. Several years later he became the Chairman of the Revolutionary Committee in the famous model Dazhai (Tachai) agricultural commune, and a member of the National People's Congress.

In Kuomintang China there were no social services to ameliorate the miserable conditions of the masses. No public health aid helped the poor when they fell sick; no unemployment pay was provided for the workless; and no old age pensions existed. Incidentally, even if there had been provision for such pensions they would rarely have needed to be paid, because the physical weakness of most of the population was such that the normal age of death among them was about 50 years. This was in remarkable contrast to the situation in nearby Hong Kong, where many Chinese were still hale and hearty when they were 70, 80 or even occasionally 90 years old.

Nor was there much opportunity for individuals among the masses to improve their lot, since hardly any schools existed for the education of children other than those of the upper and middle classes. The huge majority of the population stayed illiterate. And periodically terrible calamities struck them. Floods, droughts, insect pests or typhoons suddenly descended on this or that region, and people died of starvation in tens of thousands, hundreds of thousands and sometimes millions. No

William MacQuitty with the jovial stoker of the cremation bonfires, Shanghai

William MacQuitty writes:
After telling their nationals to leave the Yangtse Valley and the China coast, the Japanese Third Fleet assembled at Shanghai. The Great Powers requested that it should be free from hostilities, but two days later, August 6, 1937, Japanese soldiers were attacked outside the International Settlement by Chinese troops. The Japanese Navy opened fire. The Chartered Bank, where I worked, sustained two direct hits, but remained in operation throughout the hostilities and to the present day.

The worst incident occurred on August 14, 1937 when five Chinese planes flew across the International Settlement towards the Chartered Bank. Their target was a Japanese battleship on the Huangpu, but as they were met by a hail of anti-aircraft fire their aim became faulty. Two bombs fell on the Palace Hotel, now the Peace Hotel, and others fell on Nanjing Road causing horrific casualties. In the above photographs, multilated victims litter the streets where even the tar is burning.

The Japanese surrounded the International Settlement where the population had doubled with starving refugees. Each morning victims of famine and war, too many to be buried by ancient customs, were taken to waste ground and cremated. The photographs opposite show the mound of wooden coffins around naked bodies within. The stoker ladles kerosene onto the pyre.

42

government organization or transport system existed to send them food to save their lives.

All this was in vivid contrast to the luxury in which many of the Kuomintang military and civil potentates and their associates lived. I knew how extrenely well-off they were, for several of them were friends whom I used to go and see in their plutocratic homes. Several times, for example, I visited T. V. Soong in one or another of his charming houses in Hong Kong or New York as well as in China. He was the brother of the three celebrated Soong sisters who married Sun Yat-sen, H. H. Kung and Chiang Kai-shek respectively. I became fond of him, because no other millionaire whom I have known was more richly endowed with brains and charm as well as with material possessions. But in the succession of high offices which he held he did not use his immense abilities to improve the lot of his poor compatriots so much as to maintain his and his associates' own wealth, in addition to trying to solve top-level national and international economic and other problems. Of course, through centuries such practices had been customary among the rulers in not only China but many other lands round the world.

It is necessary to recall all this if one is to realize the remarkable changes which have occurred in China since 1949, and to understand why the population there became so universally worshipful of their new leader, Mao Zedong.

4 The People's Republic of China

THE PRIME AIM OF MAO ZEDONG AND HIS COLLEAGUES WHEN THEY ATTAINED POWER was to create an egalitarian Communist society throughout the whole of China. The chief purpose of this was to raise the material standard of living and to uplift the whole way of life of the then about 550,000,000 poor Chinese people. In addition the leaders deplored the feebleness which had afflicted the nation during the previous century, and were determined to restore its strength so that it would once more command high respect and exert wide influence throughout Asia and beyond.

These aims could, of course, not be swiftly achieved. To attain them the government must not only institute widespread radical social changes but also stimulate and organize agricultural, industrial and other economic developments on an immense scale. They did not favour Sun Yat-sen's idea of introducing parliamentary democracy as the means of doing all this. On the contrary, they believed that it could only be accomplished by strong authoritarian rule, which in any case was traditional in China. They simply replaced the old forms of Imperial autocracy by new ones which were described as "dictatorship of the proletariat".

I must not take space here to analyse in detail the characters and functions of the various central, provincial and local organs of government. The two supreme bodies are the Central Committee of the Communist Party and the State Council. The former decides the overall principles and major matters of national policy, and the latter is the executive authority which carries these out in practice. The State Council also takes decisions on lesser matters of policy. It is nominally responsible to the indirectly elected National People's Congress, which has legislative duties; but in fact through the thirty years before 1979 the Congress met only about half-a-dozen times for fairly short periods, and although it appointed a more regularly active Standing Committee this did not exert much influence on policy making.

45

The members of the State Council consist of a Premier, some Vice-Premiers and other Ministers, the majority of whom are members of the Communist Party's Central Committee. For instance, Hua Guofeng (Hua Kuo-feng) is now both the Chairman of the Central Committee of the Party and the Premier in the State Council. All this indicates that the Party in effect rules the country. That is so not only in the case of overall national affairs, but also at every level of regional and local affairs, where the Party's branches exercise the principal authority in guiding policies. These arrangements confirm the Article in the People's Republic's Constitution which declares that "The working class exercises leadership over the state through its vanguard, the Communist Party of China". So in spite of some touches of democratic practices enshrined in the Constitution the government is in reality an autocracy ruling in what the authorities regard as the interests of the people with their approval.

I should add here that in certain areas of the country live small populations of different ethnic types from the multitudinous Chinese. Their total collective number of individuals is now about 54,000,000. Through centuries they have practised in those regions their own native cultures. The Republic's Constitution states that all these various "minority nationalities" have "freedom to use and develop their own spoken and written languages and to preserve or reform their own customs and ways". Where the people of any of them live "in a compact community" they are given a certain amount of regional autonomy, but those areas are all "inalienable parts of the People's Republic of China" which is described as a "unitary multinational state".

During the first few years the leaders in Beijing and their officials everywhere were largely preoccupied with re-establishing effective nation-wide governmental administration, rehabilitating huge regions which had suffered devastation in the wars against the Japanese and the Kuomintang, and rescuing the national economy from a morass of inflation and other evils into which it had recently sunk. Only afterwards, in 1953, were they able to launch their initial comprehensive Five Years Plan for economic development.

In agriculture the process passed through several preliminary stages of advance. The first was the confiscation of the land everywhere from the landlords and its redistribution as countless millions of small fields to all the peasants. This encouraged hard work by those rustics in growing food and other crops. But by themselves as a multitude of separate individuals each cultivating a tiny acreage of soil with primitive hand-tools their efforts could not be anything like sufficiently productive. Co-operation between groups of them was therefore organized on a progressively broadening scale, starting among close neighbouring families, extending later to larger groups of those families, and afterwards expanding to include all the inhabitants of several adjacent villages in co-operatives. Only by such team labour could the land be farmed in an increasingly productive way which, among other results, would earn more and more capital for the purchase of the huge quantities of modern implements, agricultural machinery and other requirements, such as good fertilizers, essential to help the nation's economic growth.

In industry the authorities' plan had to start almost from scratch. Modern mills and factories existed only in the North-east and in a few cities like Shanghai and Tianjin, and on a comparatively small scale. Moreover, most of the factories that allegedly manufactured sophisticatedly mechanized products were in fact either repair workshops or plants for assembling the parts of vehicles or machinery imported from

A peasant family in Xingjiang Commune

Japan, America or elsewhere. In addition there were of course trading firms and banks, but again in very limited numbers compared with those in the highly industrialized nations elsewhere. The continuing effective management of those institutions would require for some time to come the experienced aid of their existing private owners; so for several years after 1949 they were left as those capitalists' properties in every case where the individual concerned was ready to operate them in co-operation with the government's officials and in accordance with its policies. In the same way small businesses such as shops were retained for a while by their private owners. Those loyal collaborators with the Communist regime were described as "national capitalists" and "small capitalists" respectively.

The economic development plans envisaged not only a vast extension of the productive work in the existing industrial enterprises but also the establishment of very large numbers of all sorts of new manufacturing projects. There were far too few experienced industrial experts in China to organize and guide that huge expansion. In the carrying out of their schemes from 1953 onwards the government at first received valuable help from their then Russian allies. The rulers of the already economically highly developed Soviet Union supplied them with not only considerable financial aid but also professional blue-prints, up-to-date technical know-how, a lot of modern machinery, other types of factory equipment, and thousands of skilled workers and managerial experts. Production in factories and fields alike increased quite swiftly, and on an impressive scale. But the task ahead was colossal because of the extremely backward, economically almost primitive state of affairs from which it sprang.

Some of the leaders in Beijing grew impatient, believing that if a really colossal, regimented effort were made, all their ultimate goals could be quickly reached. So in 1958 the very ambitious Great Leap Forward was launched. Through the next 2–3 years in mining and industry the nationalization of previously capitalist-owned enterprises was universally completed, and in agriculture the gigantic collectively-owned communes were established. Many government authorities felt confident that within a few more years economic advance of a magnitude comparable with that of rich nations like Japan, Britain and even the United States of America could be achieved.

Much formidable further progress was indeed made. Then two harsh blows struck the effort. One was three consecutive bad harvests in 1959, 1960 and 1961 caused by floods in some regions and droughts in others. They seriously reduced the production of not only foodstuffs but also raw materials like cotton and oils which were essential for the expeditious expansion of industrial outputs. This forced the government to devote more of its foreign exchange resources than it had planned to importing vital foodstuffs and raw materials instead of capital equipment necessary for further important industrial expansion.

However, the setback did demonstrate the success of the government's work in certain fields. Prior to 1949 such a series of natural disasters would have brought death by starvation to millions of people – yet I was told that during those three years very small numbers actually died from that cause. Because of the establishment of effectively co-ordinated nation-wide administration, and also a considerable recent extension of roads, railways and other means of communication into various previously unserved corners of the land the government were able, by rationing food in good crop areas and transporting the surpluses to badly hit regions, to distribute it nearly everywhere so that, although many suffered from malnutrition, almost everyone had enough to eat to keep them alive. It was an unprecedented event in Chinese history.

Nevertheless, I should add that the existence of trunk roads in many districts is still seriously inadequate.

The second heavy blow at China's economic expansion was the sudden withdrawal at the end of the 1950s of Russian financial and other material aid, and the recall from China of all the Soviet technicians, managers and other experts working there. Without any warning the Moscow authorities broke their promises to give such help. One result was that many large joint Soviet–Chinese projects in process of completion were halted unfinished. Numerous partly-built factories and heaps of not yet installed light and heavy machinery stood idle.

The reason for the Russians' unfriendly act was significant. It arose partly from ideological differences of outlook between those two supremely important Communist nations. This was nothing new. In earlier years, when the Russians exerted some influence in Chinese affairs through their advisers to the Kuomintang government in Guangzhou, divergencies of view had occasionally arisen between them and some leaders of the then young Chinese Communist Party about the latter's right tactical attitude toward their Kuomintang senior partners. Later a major difference of opinion grew between them about the best political and military strategy for achieving an ultimate Communist victory in China. The Russians kept insisting that it could only

Above and overleaf: A wet May Day celebration in Hangzhou

be attained by rousing rebellion among the urban workers in the cities and towns against their capitalist oppressors, as had been stated by Karl Marx. Some of the Chinese Communist leaders accepted this view, but Mao Zedong and some others disagreed with it. He urged that in Chinese circumstances the hoped-for revolution could only be accomplished by rousing the multitudes of rustic peasantry in the villages to revolt against their landlords. Of course he was right. Marx based his class-war doctrine on the situation which he knew in highly industrialized European countries where the population of industrial workers was very large. He was not so aware of the very different circumstances in an economically rather archaic land like China, where industrial development had scarcely yet begun and few urban workers existed.

When Mao's views turned out to be correct, and the Russians' advice was proved wrong, the leaders in the Kremlin were nonetheless pleased at the result, and for several years they gave the government in Beijing the extremely valuable aid which I have mentioned. Occasional disagreements arose between the two parties about this or that detail of the plans for China's economic development; but the Russians no doubt hoped, and probably expected, that their grateful comrades in weak, under-developed China would become stooges of the highly developed super-power Russia in their joint striving toward their shared aim of encouraging a world-wide Communist Revolution. However, if that was their view, they must soon have began to suspect that this could be another miscalculation by them concerning China; and I wonder whether when the dictators in Moscow realized that not only would the customarily self-confident Chinese refuse to be their puppets, but also that the substantial aid which they themselves were giving to those very able people could enable them to

49

become powerful Communist rivals to the Russian nation, the latter prospect was another reason why they suddenly withdrew their aid. If so, it was in a way an example of history repeating itself. The centuries old mutual enmity between those two large neighbouring states in the Far East revived, not so much on ideological as on nationalist grounds.

So of a sudden the Chinese were left on their economic own before they themselves possessed anything like enough know-how, practical experience, trained workers, skilled technicians, modern equipment or other requirements to accomplish quite quickly their gigantic task. In those times they received extremely little effective help from any other external nation. From the moment of the Communists' victory in 1949 the United States of America had imposed an embargo on all American exports to and imports from China; and some of the democratic European nations and Japan had partially conformed with that policy. So although they engaged in some foreign trade, the Chinese were forced to depend largely on their own resources.

They resolved to become self-reliant. And although they lacked a lot of practical up-to-date experience in industrial and agricultural productive techniques they were blessed with clever inventive minds. Partly by copying foreign tools, machines and other equipment which they already possessed, and partly by devising improvements in the effectiveness of these they produced ever larger quantities and better qualities of the machinery that they needed. For a long time to come they would nevertheless possess only a tiny fraction of the sophisticated mechanical implements which they required; but they commanded a substitute instrument of immense creative power – mass human manual labour. Scores of millions of workers and peasants were mobilized to perform tens of thousands of varied tasks. For example, at the peak period of the construction of a large new reservoir near the Ming Tombs not far from Beijing 100,000 men and women workers, peasants, soldiers, university students and volunteers helped to build it, mostly by hand. Incidentally, among the volunteers now and then helping to dig the reservoir with hand shovels were Mao Zedong, Zhou Enlai and General Zhu De. The reservoir's barrage stretched 627 metres long, 179 metres wide at its base, 29 metres high, and $7\frac{1}{2}$ metres broad at its entry top, with a capacity to store 82,000,000 cubic metres of water for distribution along freshly dug canals to irrigate the fields of eight adjacent agricultural communes. Yet it took only 160 days between January and June 1958 to complete, for haste was necessary to avoid a risk of autumn floods pouring down and damaging it. As part of the same water conservation scheme more than 4,000,000 trees were planted over the near-by hills.

Actually that reservoir did not turn out to be a success because it was poorly designed. But it was just one typical, average-sized project. Many irrigation, afforestation, electric power and other schemes were successfully constructed on an even vaster scale, whilst countless smaller ones were effectively created all over the country. For instance, by 1962 nearly 200 entirely new industrial towns containing huge iron and steel works, oil refineries or various other types of factories, plus residential housing estates, shopping centres, theatres, hospitals, sports stadiums and other amenities were built in previously sparsely populated places.

I viewed some of them during the next visit that I paid to China in the autumn of that year. They had to be seen to be believed. I sometimes pinched myself to make sure that I was awake when I gazed at a colossal new metropolis raised to a considerable extent by human manual labour.

Modern irrigation works at Shaoshan

During a month of extensive travels in cities, towns and countrysides then I observed much evidence of the progress being made in all sorts of national activities. And I discussed the current situation with numerous administrators, workers, peasants, students, university professors and others.

My most important conversations were those which I held with Premier Zhou Enlai and Foreign Minister Marshal Chen Yi. By good chance they and I had become cordial friends during earlier meetings in other countries through the previous few years. Our discussions in 1962 continued through three days after my return to Beijing from wide journeys in various different regions of the land.

Zhou Enlai opened one of them with a characteristically genial remark. "You've seen many parts of China in the last four weeks", he said, "including several that we ourselves haven't seen lately. Tell us your impressions. And tell us first what you think we're doing wrong, not what you think we're doing right. We can move on to that other topic later."

I made my criticisms, and we discussed them. In the course of the talks the two

53

Duck farming and fish farming at Wuxi Commune

Ministers expressed some pleasure at what had been achieved in China since 1949; but they were far from satisfied, and still less complacent. They remarked that through the last dozen years the government had made only a small beginning in its huge tasks. Although, for example, as a result of the start of an uplift in the national economy the material standard of living of the hundreds of millions of people had been distinctly raised, in many cases that was not saying much! Nevertheless the earlier conditions of life of an overwhelming majority of them had been so appallingly poor that even a small improvement – such as several bowls of rice instead of only one to eat each day – seemed to those humble folk to be substantial. But there was still a long, long way to go before it became anything like adequate. The government and whole nation must continue to strive hard and long.

The Ministers spoke about the recent Great Leap Forward, describing its considerable successes but also its partial failures. They said that there were three main reasons for the failures. First, the succession of bad harvests had gravely prejudiced advance. Second, the withdrawal of Russian aid crippled progress. (My informants did not mention the Russians by name, merely referring to them as "a supposedly friendly power" – knowing perfectly well that I would understand of whom they were talking.) And the third reason that they gave for the failures was some serious mistakes made by the Chinese themselves in planning. They told me that one cause of these mistakes was that some of their colleagues in the government (whom they again refrained from naming) had been much too optimistic about the pace at which the modernisation of the nation's agricultural and industrial economy could be completely achieved.

They talked candidly about the mistakes. A major error was that (only partly because they had counted on receiving continuing Russian help) in their industrial planning they had tried to progress too far too fast, building a much greater diversity of factories than they could gear into production at more or less the same time. They had not been careful enough to select practical priorities, and would now have to close many of the less urgent new plants until a time arrived when these could be put into effective production. This did not mean that those buildings and their machines would be wasted; they would be kept in good trim so that in due course they could begin to play their parts in the nation's economic progress. Soldierly Chen Yi described the situation in military terms, saying "We launched our offensive on too big a scale, and captured so many positions that we cannot at present hold them all. We've got to make a tactical retreat for a while, abandoning those which it's for the time being unnecessary to defend, and concentrating our energies on strengthening our grip on the vital posts which we must continue to command. Later we shall launch another offensive and recapture the positions from which we're temporarily withdrawing."

Another blunder was that some industries which depended on agricultural crops such as cotton or soya beans for their raw materials were expanded too fast, owing to miscalculations about the time it would take to produce sufficient continuous supplies of those crops. Indeed, a major overall error had been a failure to realize to what a great extent agriculture must be the basis of the whole national economy, and how considerably the effective expansion of secondary industry in general would depend on an immense related expansion of agriculture. One result of the above two mis-calculations had been that far too many people had been transferred from the rural areas to live and work in the cities and towns. They were now being returned to their villages in the countrysides.

A further error had been that in certain workshops the production of spare parts and auxiliary equipment like repair tools for the heavy machinery made for use in the same factories had been insufficient, with the result that some of the machinery was now standing helplessly idle.

The Ministers spoke equally frankly about mistakes which had originally been made in the establishment of the agricultural communes. One was that at the start many of them were much too large for efficient management, having populations of three or four score thousands of people. The sensible number should usually (though not always) be considerably less, and much smaller in certain types of country such as highland areas.

Another error was that at the beginning too much bureaucratic dictation by Communist Party cadres in the town headquarters of communes had been imposed on the peasants at village level about the planning and carrying-out of the communes' production programmes – an attempt at excessive regimentation which those latter strong, and often locally much more practically experienced farming characters resented and resisted. Now distinctly more autonomy in decision-making, within certain major overall limits, was being conceded to the village teams; and this was helping rather than hindering the attainment of the government's very big agricultural production targets.

The Ministers mentioned some other errors which had since been corrected. In particular they said that when the communes were first created private ownership by individuals of even tiny plots of land in the collectively-owned farms had been abolished.

This had caused discontent, and tended to weaken the rustics' will to work hard in the publicly-owned fields. Now small garden-size plots had been restored to every family, on which they could grow their own vegetables and keep a few chickens, pigs and rabbits. This had helped to stimulate really energetic toil throughout the communes.

In that connection Zhou told me that some of their colleagues in the government who had been over-optimistic about the pace at which the nation's immense economic development could be achieved had also been over-sanguine about how quickly an ideal, completely egalitarian Communist society could be established in China with the willing consent of the people. Those comrades had expected that the population would readily accept that everyone should receive equal pay for whatever quantity and quality of work they performed, and that they would all labour very hard and well because their prime purpose would be to serve their fellow men. This was the reason why those wishful thinkers had initially abolished all privately owned plots of land in the communes, and why some of them even anticipated that before long all the workers in industry, peasants in agriculture and intellectuals in professional occupations would be happy to receive similar material returns for their varied activities. They therefore urged that material incentives for better work should be abolished. They were of course wrong – idealists who misjudged the human nature of their fellow Chinese. Zhou agreed that the eventual achievement of such a model egalitarian society should be the government's ultimate aim, but he felt that it could only be approached slowly by a gradual step-by-step process. It would first be necessary to educate the masses in the ethical rectitude of an egalitarian state in which everyone was inspired by a wish to devote himself or herself altruistically to the service of their whole community. This could not be done quickly, and in the meantime the authorities must be pragmatic realists, recognizing that the people would remain for a considerable time typical human beings endowed with a mixture of good and bad qualities. One of the weaknesses in the characters of a great majority of them was a desire to serve themselves first, and to help other individuals or groups only afterwards. So in order to stimulate truly hard and able work by the whole population – which was essential if the modernization of China's agriculture, industry and other important interests were to be achieved reasonably soon – the temptation of material rewards must, for the present at least, be offered to the workers and peasants. Hence the existing system in industry where eight different grades of workers were paid respectively eight different rates of wages, from the most highly skilled performers like chief engineers at the top, through a succession of less distinguished types of operators to the least capable labourers at the bottom. And individuals who performed especially good work in their grade not only received additional pay, but were also publicly acclaimed as heroic model workers. In agriculture, too, all the peasants in a commune were not paid exactly the same wages. Each and every man's or woman's monthly pay was calculated according to the amount of ploughing, harrowing, sowing or other effective work that he or she accomplished throughout that period.

Zhou Enlai and Chen Yi both hoped that, as the years passed, more and more progress towards the creation of a truly egalitarian society could be made by periodic narrowings of the gaps between those various rates of pay, until perhaps the differences could eventually disappear. In the meantime material incentives must continue to be offered to the workers and peasants.

Reverting to the principal aim of the Great Leap Forward, the two Ministers told

Mother and child coolly appraise the photographer

me that their colleagues in the government who indulged in wishful thinking had reckoned that a fully economically developed Chinese state, providing all the necessities, comforts and amenities needed by its colossal population, could be created "in our lifetime" – which meant within about a dozen years. Now those dreamers realized that this was a gross miscalculation. Zhou Enlai and Chen Yi expressed to me the view that it would take:

(i) about 10 years for agriculture throughout a self-reliant China to be expanded to a point where it produced sufficient quantities, varieties and qualities of essential foodstuffs to feed properly the entire population;

(ii) between 30 and 40 years to develop mining and industries on a nationwide scale which produced sufficient capital and consumer goods to meet the people's and nation's other material necessities; and

(iii) between 80 and 100 years before conditions could be fully created which would give China's vast population the same high standard of living as peoples in the most developed Western countries enjoyed.

For this reason they wished China to be left in peace for the next two or three generations, so that its successive governments could concentrate the nation's energies and resources on moving steadily towards the achievement of that ultimate state of affairs.

Zhou emphasized that one reason why the process would be so protracted was that China must become as entirely as possible self-supporting. Its people could not depend on help from other nations. First the Americans' boycott of any trade whatever with China which had continued ever since the Communists came to power in 1949, and later the Russians' sudden withdrawal of all their aid had made him and his colleagues realize that the Chinese must to a very considerable extent "go it alone." He told me that they would gladly trade with friendly nations like Britain and others who had already provided them with useful factory machinery and equipment, but only to a marginal extent. As many as possible of the nation's agricultural, industrial and other requirements must be produced by itself. Nevertheless, with a view to developing that ability they would like to learn from Western nations a lot about their modern technological means of production.

He commented that one of the causes of the slow-down in their rate of progress following the withdrawal of Russian help was an unexpected shortage of maturely expert technicians in many of their large industrial plants and related works. A very inadequate number of sufficiently experienced men and women of that kind existed at present in the Chinese population itself. In their new steel works, machine-making factories and other such enterprises they did have many well trained young engineers and other technicians who were showing great promise, but who had not yet had long enough practical experience to develop their great talents to the full. They would be excellent leaders in their important spheres of work ten or fifteen years hence, but in the meantime they lacked anything like enough practical know-how in their supremely responsible jobs. Zhou remarked that during my recent visits to many industrial undertakings in various parts of the country I had no doubt noticed that none of the chief engineers or other such principal workers in charge of vitally important departments of production were older than, at most, their late thirties.

I replied that I had indeed been struck by the youthful appearances of everyone holding those highly responsible posts – so struck that I had ventured to ask each one of them his or her age. And I added that what he had just said to me was not entirely correct. It was true that all of those several dozen individuals whom I had met were in their lower, middle or late thirties – with a solitary exception. One of them was 45 years old.

Zhou raised his eyebrows in surprise, and with a merry twinkle in his eyes commented that I knew more about contemporary China than he did. He thanked me for teaching him something about it.

Then he stated that the somewhat inexperienced youthfulness of almost every one of the technicians whom I had met was partly due to the fact that before 1949 only an extremely small minority of the population in China had received any education in schools and universities or polytechnics. An overwhelming majority of the people could not then even read or write. Now the numbers who were literate were rapidly growing, but most of those individuals were still in their late teens or early twenties.

He added that the government gave careful consideration as to what the priorities should be for the kinds of professional or technical training which the up-and-coming college students should receive. One of China's present difficulties, for example, was its great shortage of good physicists who could conduct constructive researches into the development of nuclear energy. The education of these would be a top priority.

During my extensive travels earlier that month I had observed with my own eyes many of the conditions described by Zhou Enlai and Chen Yi. Among others I caught sights of the still very simple methods of agricultural production employed by the peasants. For instance, wherever new crops of wheat were being sowed the land was ploughed with antique single-blade wooden ploughs. These were usually drawn by a water-buffalo or an ox in front whilst the ploughman grasping the handles behind guided the implement along a furrow. But quite often human beings performed the function of those animals, one or more men or women – sometimes as many as half-a-dozen, depending on the toughness of the soil – being harnessed to tug the plough forward. Many other labourers toiled similarly along the country roads. Although usually a horse, donkey, mule or occasionally an ox pulled each heavily-laden small cart, quite often one, two or three human beings were harnessed instead by ropes to a vehicle, and hauled it onward. Only rather rarely did a new phenomenon called a motor van roll into sight doing that freight-carrying job.

I could describe many other related features in the rural scenery reminiscent of the ancient China which I had witnessed everywhere during my previous visits to the country, and much of which still survived. Numerous peasants, for instance, trotted along the lanes carrying lengthy shoulder poles with a heavily-laden basket dangling from each end. But one feature in particular had changed since a dozen years earlier. None of the people now looked thin, half-starved and dressed in rags. All the men, women and children everywhere appeared physically robust, hale and hearty; and they all wore neatly tailored, if rather dull, universally standardized clothing.

Other features in the landscapes also indicated the significant new developments which were occurring. Since my last visit many, many new irrigation canals had been cut through the land to assist the growth of crops; in appropriate areas tree-planting had evidently been recently organized on a widespread scale, for avenues, copses and sometimes forests of new young trees were sprouting; and in many regions the farmlands under cultivation had been enormously extended, almost every possible square inch of ground being used for this or that kind of agricultural production. And on previously wild hillsides the slopes had been cut into terraces like wide, high staircases of tilled soil growing orchards of fruit or other kinds of foodstuffs. One of the communes that I visited was the celebrated model one at Dazhai, where all these developments had been very impressively accomplished.

In the cities and towns I likewise witnessed a mixture of the very old and the new China. A typical example of the former were the numerous elderly and middle-aged women who hobbled along the streets on "bound" feet. A confrontation of the two eras appeared in roads where rows of old, still inhabited shacks existed along one side, whilst rows of new houses had been built along the other side. And signs of the more modern China were the numerous new factories with smoke belching from their tall chimneys, indicating their busily active productivity. At the same time here and there I noticed such buildings standing empty, with untended machinery lying on the ground around them – bits of evidence either of the miscalculations made by too zealous planners during the Great Leap Forward, or else of the obstruction inflicted on industrial development by the Russians' precipitate withdrawal of aid.

Perhaps more important than anything else in the changing state of affairs was its effect on the living conditions of the multitudes of ordinary people. The improvements in their circumstances did not spring only from the somewhat higher pay which the nation's economic growth gave them in return for their labours. In addition, as soon as the new government came into power it had begun to introduce various previously non-existent welfare services to help them. Creches and nursery schools instituted in every factory and village for the care of infants whose parents were working through much of each day, a public health service which established medical clinics and hospitals available for everyone throughout the country, and the payment of old-age pensions to elderly industrial workers after their retirement were typical examples of these. Nor did the government's education policy consist only of a steady immense increase in the numbers of primary and middle schools throughout the country which would as soon as possible enable all the children to attend the former and a very large proportion of them to attend the latter. In addition an expansion of polytechnics and universities which would enable many more youngsters to receive higher training and education took place. And the authorities organized large numbers of adult education classes to teach countless older, illiterate workers and peasants how to read, write and achieve other useful accomplishments.

I gained many impressions of the results of the changes in the people's ways of life in talks which I held with all sorts of folk at their work or in their homes. Here I shall mention four representative cases: those of a rural peasant family, an urban worker's family, a single young woman and a retired old man.

The peasants lived in a commune near Nanjing. I believe their circumstances were about average. Numerous rustic families whom I met were rather better off than they were, whilst others were somewhat less so. Before describing their particular circumstances I should mention that the annual revenue earned by each individual commune differed from that earned by others, not simply because of their differing sizes but also because of the different financial returns which they each gained from their collective production of various types of crops. As a result the average rate of pay received by the peasants varied somewhat from commune to commune. To illustrate how those collective farms' financial affairs were managed I shall quote the figures which were given to me in a typical one. I was told that 6.1% of its total earnings each year were paid in tax to the government, 6% went into its capital and welfare fund, something between 20% and 30% (varying from year to year according to current requirements) was kept to pay for seeds, tools and other production needs, and all the rest was distributed in wages to the peasants. An instalment was paid to each individual each month, in accordance with the amount of his or her labour through that period, and the balance was given to them when the commune's annual accounts were completed.

The father of the family whose circumstances I shall describe was a lean, wiry, handsome middle-aged fellow. He, his wife, their four young children and his mother lived in a small cottage. Before 1949 he had worked for a landlord. All the crops from the fields where he and his fellow labourers then toiled had to be handed over to their master, and in return he (like the others) received enough simple food to feed himself for about six months each year. He was compelled to do wood-cutting and other odd jobs in all his spare time to scrape up enough cash to keep himself alive for the rest of the year. So for a long time he could not afford to keep a wife, and remained single. A couple of years before 1949, however, he married a peasant girl who also worked at various jobs which earned her enough to feed herself. They lodged in a tiny straw shack owned by their landlord.

"If we'd had four children in those days" he remarked to me, "we'd all have starved".

He and his wife now earned from their work in the commune's fields and from the sale of vegetables and eggs produced on their private plot of ground rather more than enough money to supply all the family's necessities. This was helped by the extra food which a brace of ducks, a couple of pigs, several rabbits and enough hens to lay 5 or 6 eggs a day on their plot provided. Two years ago he had saved sufficient cash to buy himself a pedal-bicycle, and a year ago he had purchased a transistor radio. Recently he had bought a lot of bricks and, with the help of neighbours, had built the new family cottage, which contained two living rooms, a kitchen, a toilet and a backyard. He was its owner, without any need to pay rent. The rooms were simply but adequately furnished with tables, chairs and beds; the kitchen was quite well stocked with pots and pans; and the cupboards contained a goodly supply of clothes, blankets and quilts – all his own property. The man and his wife both wore wrist-watches which they had recently bought, and they were now considering what their next major purchase should be. It would probably be a sewing-machine.

The pair paid the equivalent of thirty English pence a year as health insurance, in return for which they and their dependants all got free medicine and medical care in the local clinic, as well as in the commune's hospital when necessary. Their two elder children received free education in the village primary school. The two others were still too young to attend classes, and were cared for by his mother whilst he and his wife were working in the fields.

"All this was unimaginable in the old days", he commented with a smile of intense pleasure.

Incidentally, he had helped several of his neighbours to build new cottages for their families in a similar way as they had helped him. That sort of co-operation was being encouraged in many communes.

The industrial workers whose circumstances I shall sketch were weavers in one of three recently built cotton-mills in Beijing. The family consisted of an elderly married couple, their son and daughter-in-law, and the latter pair's six-months-old baby. They lived in an apartment consisting of two rooms plus a kitchen and a toilet.

The grandparents had both worked in a textile factory in Shanghai until the early 1950s, when they came to Beijing as skilled workers to train the inexperienced recruits in the new mill. The old man told me of the changes in their life "since Liberation in 1949". Before that the shifts in textile mills – as in other factories – had continued for 12 hours each day; but immediately after Liberation they were reduced to 8 hours. Three such shifts in succession kept the mill productive throughout every 24 hours. His wage in Shanghai had been scarcely enough to buy his own food, and his wife

Opposite : Concrete boats, which are virtually indestructible, are made at the Cement Boat Factory in Wuxi

had to work to feed herself. He did extra jobs after his long daily labour in order to earn extra money to buy food for their then young boy. The fare was extremely meagre in quantity and poor in quality, and prices were so unstable that often they had to do with too little even of that. Now his wage was more than enough to buy an ample variety of good foodstuffs for both his wife and himself; and so she need not work. Nevertheless she would have done so in the new mill if she were physically fit; but the conditions of work in Shanghai had been such that she contracted an ailment which gradually became incurable because there was then no provision for medical treatment for workers. Now they enjoyed free medical care, and their doctor had advised her to cease factory work.

Their living quarters in Shanghai had been a hovel. He remarked to me that the apartment which they now shared with their son, daughter-in-law and grandchild was "very modest, but luxurious in comparison". The younger couple also worked in the same mill, and the joint wages of the three workers in the family gave them considerable sums to spend on non-necessities. Moreover, whereas in earlier times the senior pair would have become entirely dependent on their son in their old age, now they would be independent because on retirement at 60 years old in his case and at 55 years in his wife's they would each receive an adequate pension.

Elderly people were not only cared for nowadays by a pension. Those who wished could retire to an Old Folks' Home, thousands of which had been established all over the country since 1949. I shall return to that topic later. First I shall mention my third representative case: an unmarried member of the young generation. She was a sturdy, pretty girl aged 20 who worked as an attendant on a railway train in which I travelled. Her name was Bai Zhu (Pai Chu), which being interpreted means "Hundred Pearls". When I asked her what her ambition in life was, she replied that she wished she could be a Frontier Guard defending her motherland "against Imperialist enemies". Girls, however, were not admitted to those units, and so she had tried to become an air-pilot and parachutist instead. Unfortunately on examination her eyesight proved to be defective, and she therefore could not qualify as a pilot. She then chose to start work on the railway. She lived with her parents at one end of the long line, and shared a free dormitory (run by the authorities) with other girl attendants when they stayed for nights away from home. Their food was also provided free. Her basic wage was 37 yuan a month, but she received extra pay for each journey, and her monthly income usually worked out at about 50 yuan.

"That's much more money than I can spend", she remarked with a merry laugh.

I shall interpret the yuan into its then pounds sterling value later.

Now I shall turn to a single unwedded representative of the old generation. In Fushun I visited a rather stately mansion which had been built a few years ago in a spacious garden as an Old Men's Home. It was inhabited by 120 ancient bachelors. A typical member of the fraternity was a fellow aged 78 with a wrinkled face, narrowly slanting bright eyes and a long straggly goatee-beard. In reply to my questions he told me the story of his life.

His parents had both died when he was 6 years old, leaving him a helpless orphan. For the next several years he was a beggar wandering through the streets, until he got a job as an early teen-age coal-miner. Conditions of work in the mine were appalling, and his rate of pay was so low and the employment so irregular that he could never afford to get married. That state of affairs continued through about three decades, after which he was thrown permanently out of work. Once more he became a beggar. He had given up hope of continued existence – when suddenly "Liberation arrived". It brought him a pension, residence in the Old Men's Home, and a fresh prospect of life.

Gently stroking his beard he remarked, "I wouldn't be alive today, I would have died of starvation years ago, if it were not for Chairman Mao and the Communist Party".

I commented that he looked so fit that he would probably live for another 20 years.

His eyes lit up, and he grinned gleefully as he exclaimed, "I would like to live another twenty years to see the growth of socialism in China".

He had of course been taught the Communist Party catch-phrases; nevertheless he spoke them spontaneously from not only a full belly but also a full heart. He told me that his pension was more than he needed for his board, lodging, clothes and other necessities. When I enquired what he spent his spare cash on, he chortled and answered that he liked first a little drink of wine, and afterwards bought seeds for a collection of pot-plants which he kept in his bedroom. He added that his "comrades" in the House enjoyed various other recreations, such as breeding goldfish.

Looking around the company in the Home I thought that but for Chairman Mao quite a number of its inmates would have been rotting in graveyards that afternoon instead of sipping wine, growing pot-plants, breeding goldfish, tending song-birds in cages, playing chess and pursuing other genial hobbies in the autumn sunshine.

I must mention another individual. He was a representative of a very different section of the population, a "national capitalist". For several years before 1949 he had been the owner of a woollen factory in Tianjin. After the Communist Revolution his expert experience as its director was greatly needed by the government authorities in the conduct of their industrial programme, and for a while they left it in his private ownership provided that he managed it in conformity with their policy, and indeed instructions. In 1954 it became a joint venture between them and him. In our conversation he told me that they made a correct assessment of the value of the property when they took it over, and gave him an equivalent sum in the form of capital investment in it. Immediately afterwards the factory was greatly expanded and improved, the government providing all the new capital needed for that. And ever since then he had continued to be its active and influential general manager, although the government decided its policy in consultation with him and a group of directors, one of whom was a member of his old senior staff whilst others were representatives appointed by the Minister responsible.

In addition to his pay of 400 yuan a month as the manager he was guaranteed a fixed interest of 5% each year on his share of the capital, whatever the profits or losses of the factory might be from year to year. And he had been assured that he would continue to receive that extra payment for a few more years, by which time the powers-that-be calculated that he would have been given back the money which they had in effect taken from him.

These arrangements had enabled him and his family to continue living in their quite large house attended by all their old servants. Nevertheless in various ways their existence was less luxurious than it had previously been. Unlike the four other cases that I have described, their material standard of living had therefore been lowered since 1949. He explained to me that he had in fact lost a great deal of money because of his deprivation of the large profits made each year in the factory. But he added that he

65

was glad at the change in China. This was partly because he was pleased to see the working people enjoying a better way of life, but mostly because the new government were regaining for the Chinese nation a high regard all round the world which it had previously lacked. With evident sincerity – but perhaps also a touch of a sentiment indoctrinated into him – he said that whereas he used to feel rather ashamed of being "a Chinaman" (as he and his compatriots used to be called, with a hint of contempt, by the rulers of the Foreign Concessions in those times) he now felt proud of being a Chinese.

A large number of other pristine rich tycoons were performing similar duties and being treated in a similar way as national capitalists.

One of the government's aims was to lessen the great measure of separation which had previously existed between the urban and the rural populations, and to encourage familiar contacts between them which would promote a real sense of intimate and friendly unity throughout the nation. I learned of a typical way in which they were doing this soon after my arrival in the country. During the long train journey from the south to Beijing my guide was a government official who had welcomed me in Guangzhou. He worked in the Ministry of Foreign Affairs in Beijing. A young man in his early thirties, he had a wife and three children. His wife also worked in the capital, in an Institute concerned with international matters.

He told me that he and she had Sundays off, and in addition got holidays on days such as the Chinese New Year, the National Day and one or two other special occasions. Otherwise they had no vacations. However, throughout a month each year they went together to do manual labour in an agricultural commune, where they lived and toiled with the villagers. This gave them four weeks of rest from mental office work, and so was a sort of holiday, which they greatly enjoyed. Indeed, he commented that if his tasks in the Ministry were slacker he would be inclined to stay and work with the peasants in the fields for more than a month. Among other benefits, the experience enabled him to be in touch with those rural people and to get to know them. With a smile he remarked that his rustic hosts told him that he was "not good, but also not bad" at farm labour, and that he improved steadily at it after the initial few days.

It was compulsory for him and all the other civil servants under 46 years old, not only in his Ministry but also in all the other Government Departments, to do this month's work in a commune every year. The same applied to numerous other intellectuals engaged in professional or other activities in the cities and towns. Only individuals among them who were suffering from some physical unfitness were exempted from these annual periods of agricultural labour. Nor was it obligatory only for adults to do it. Especially at harvest-times the school children and college students marched in large groups into the country to join the peasants in their labours. I shall return to that latter aspect of the subject in a later chapter.

So the authorities in Beijing were endeavouring to create a truly united, classless society of every section of the people throughout the country.

5 China's Foreign Policy

DURING MY DAYS OF TALKS WITH ZHOU ENLAI AND CHEN YI WE DISCUSSED VARIOUS aspects of the current international situation.

In that connection I should mention that I had first met those two distinguished Chinese in 1955, when an aeroplane in which they were flying from China to attend a conference in Indonesia unexpectedly had to alight in Singapore for a while because of a need for refuelling after stormy weather further north. I was then still Britain's Commissioner General in South East Asia, and I went to the airport to greet the surprising visitors. We had a genial chat before they were able to rise into the skies again after their aircraft had been fully serviced.

At that time the "cold war" between the United States of America with its Western allies on one side and Soviet Russia with its Communist allies on the other was being vehemently waged. The conference to which the Chinese Ministers and their delegation were flying was the first international gathering of non-aligned nations who adopted a neutral attitude in that conflict. President Sukarno of Indonesia would preside over it in Bandung in Java, and the two most important statesmen there would be the Prime Minister of India, Jawarhalal Nehru, and the Prime Minister of China, Zhou Enlai. Although India was a cordial partner of Britain (a "cold war" ally of the U.S.A.) in the Commonwealth, and although China was a fellow-Communist state with Russia, those two pre-eminent Asian nations were both neutral. Under Zhou Enlai's guidance Mao Zedong's government was pursuing the non-aligned foreign policy which was to give it steadily increasing influence among the "third world" nations in international affairs.

Because of their similar outlooks on that extremely important issue, through several years both before and after the Bandung Conference Nehru of democratic India and Zhou of totalitarian China became close collaborators in developing the policies of

67

their governments regarding external problems. Now and then Nehru went to Beijing or Zhou went to Delhi for discussions together, in the course of which they formulated the famous Five Principles for achieving Peaceful Co-existence between the peoples of different nations, races, cultures and political ideologies round the world.

I always had a talk with Zhou Enlai, sometimes accompanied by Chen Yi, when he came to Delhi in the second half of the 1950s and in 1960, after I had become Britain's High Commissioner in India. Later my friendship with them both grew strong when Chen Yi was the leader of the Chinese delegation and I was the leader of the British delegation throughout a long and difficult but eventually successful International Conference held in Geneva through much of 1961 and 1962 to try to end the hot war then being fought in Laos between rival pro-Western and pro-Communist Laotian factions, with American and Russian aid to each respectively.

Thereby hangs a tale. Chen Yi and I shared a fondness for certain spare time pleasures. One was discussing beautiful ancient Chinese works of art. Another was eating meals of several courses of deliciously tasty Chinese food. One evening during a conversation whilst we were guzzling one of those dinners we discovered that our birthdays both occurred in August. The next exchange of sentences revealed that those anniversaries both happened to be on the 17th day of that month. And our following swap of information disclosed that we had both been born on that date in the year 1901. Our ages were identical. Although we were conceived by different parents and had originally opened our eyes on opposite sides of the Earth we were twins!

From that moment we regarded each other as brothers; and our often helpful diplomatic co-operation in difficult periods of the conference negotiations steadily enriched our friendship. Chen Yi was a charming, jovial man, highly talented as both a soldier and a statesman.

Incidentally, as the leader of the British delegation at Geneva I was also one of the conference's two co-Chairmen, the other being the leader of the Russian delegation, Georgi Pushkin. He was a very able, genial and constructively co-operative colleague whom I very much liked and admired.

My visit to China in 1962 was made a few months after the conference ended. I went there as a guest of the Chinese government, invited by Zhou Enlai and Chen Yi.

During my talks with them in Beijing they spoke with pleasure of the rather friendly relations existing between our two countries. They said that they and their comrades had deeply appreciated the British government's early recognition of the People's Republic of China after its creation in 1949, and the establishment of our Diplomatic Mission then in Beijing. But they regretted that we also maintained a Consulate in Taiwan as if that isle were a separate state. Our latter act was the reason why they still insisted that our Mission in Beijing and theirs in London could not be headed by an Ambassador, but must have the lesser status of being presided over by a "Chargé d'Affaires".

Then, with clear sincerity, Zhou said that although Britain had become economically, militarily and diplomatically much weaker than it used to be, and although certain other nations were now more powerful, the Chinese leaders would rather listen to the opinions of us British on international affairs, and sometimes be influenced by them, than to those of any other nation round the globe. We knew the peoples of numerous diverse nationalities and races more intimately than anyone else did, because of our

Malcolm MacDonald with Zhou Enlai

close associations with many of them distributed across all the continents and seas throughout the last century or two. He stated that we had shown a better understanding of them and a truer friendliness towards them than any other Western nation. We had foreseen our Colonial subjects' growing desire for political freedom, and had anticipated more wisely than any other old Imperial power the changes which would occur all round the world in the twentieth century. The most notable piece of evidence of this (he commented) was our almost wholly peaceful guidance of our earlier Empire of dependent colonies into a Commonwealth of independent nations. The Commonwealth was an admirable partnership of peoples of many different colours, creeds and cultures, founded on a basis of equality between them all. He hoped the Commonwealth would continue to grow ever greater in size, partly because this would mean that Britain's influence in world affairs could remain widespread.

I said, half jestingly, that I regretted that the two super-powers in the present-day world were the comparatively young, inexperienced American and Russian nations, and that I wished the pair of major powers could be the more maturely sage Chinese and Scots nations. Zhou laughed, and commented that if he thought there should be any super-powers at all he would agree with me; but he thought that no such masterful states should exist. All the diverse nations should have an equal say in the settlement of human problems.

Malcolm MacDonald with his "twin" Marshall Chen Yi in 1962

The two Ministers analysed to me in considerable detail their government's policy in international affairs. They said that its broad nature was summed up in the Five Principles which Nehru and Zhou had published in a joint statement following some of their talks in Delhi several years earlier. Those principles should guide relations not only between India and China but also between all nations. They advocated mutual respect for each other's territorial integrity and sovereignty, non-aggression against one another, non-interference in each other's internal affairs, mutually advantageous equality of status, and peaceful co-existence helped by economic co-operation between them all.

My companions said that if those principles were universally carried out in practice, they could form a firm foundation for world-wide peace. They would banish fears that certain nations felt for their security which some of the existing quarrellings kept alive. The Chinese, for example, felt apprehensive regarding the intentions towards them of certain apparently hostile peoples. That was why the government in Beijing decided that they must maintain strong military forces. Those forces were kept in full training purely for defensive purposes. If China was attacked by a foreign aggressor, they would of course counter-attack with all the strength at their command; but otherwise their soldiers, airmen and sailors would not join in any wars.

I felt convinced of the sincerity of their government's desire for peaceful co-existence with all other nations, including those with different political ideologies and social systems from their own. Apart from other considerations, this was in China's own national self-interest. As I described in the previous chapter, in our talks Zhou Enlai and Chen Yi told me that it would take vast, economically extremely backward China about 10 years to become reasonably self-supporting in agriculture, between 30 and 40 years for its industrial development to reach a similar state of affairs, and around 80 to 100 years for its economic progress to enable the Chinese population to enjoy a standard of living comparable with that of the peoples in highly developed Western lands. The two Ministers emphasized that the steady attainment of those aims must be the first priority of successive governments in Beijing through the next several decades, that any serious distraction from it must be avoided, and that therefore they hoped that international peace would prevail for a long time to come.

I received a dramatic indication of their earnest wish for this in a talk which I had with Chen Yi as soon as I returned to Beijing from my travels in other parts of China. During those journeys I was isolated from all the news of events occurring elsewhere, and so was ignorant of what was happening in other parts of the world. With a gleam of delight in his eyes Chen Yi immediately told me of one staggering event that had just occurred – the episode in which the Russians had promptly decided to drop their plan to establish a missile base in Cuba when President Kennedy in Washington issued a public warning that if the plan proceeded the Americans would take strong action against the countries concerned. The evident joy with which Chen Yi told me of this victory for capitalist America against communist Russia indicated the Chinese government's immense relief that the danger of an outbreak of a World War had been averted.

The Chinese were generally honouring the policy of peaceful co-existence not only in words but also in deeds. It was true that they were giving support in the form of military weapons and perhaps also some troops to the Vietminh regime in the war being waged in next-door Vietnam. When I asked Zhou Enlai and Chen Yi about this they said that it was an act of precautionary Chinese self-defence against the strongly growing American and other foreign military assistance being given to the South Vietnamese, which might be the prelude to an attack on China itself. I shall return to that subject later.

Wherever possible the Chinese government had settled outstanding frontier disputes with neighbouring countries by peaceful, mutually give-and-take negotiations. They had done this successfully in the cases of Afghanistan, Nepal and Burma, and were in the process of doing so with Pakistan.

For years they had striven to reach a similar accord with the Indian authorities, but with no success. The two governments disagreed about the ownership of the considerable Aksayqin (Aksai Chin) region along part of their western border and also about a lengthy area south of the so-called MacMahon Line further east. A diplomatic quarrel about these had been simmering through a few years, with just occasional little military skirmishes between small bodies of troops of the two sides. Then, following a shooting incident in a district of the disputed eastern region, some fighting occurred, and a real war threatened to break out. This crisis had erupted a few days before I arrived in Beijing at the end of my wide travels in China.

It was, of course, one of the subjects which Zhou Enlai, Chen Yi and I discussed. Our exchanges of views about it were characteristically frank. At their opening Zhou said that he fully understood why the British government was giving diplomatic support to India against China in the conflict, for India was a fellow-member of our Commonwealth of Nations, so we naturally gave it that support. He added that two days ago he had learned that we were giving India not only moral but also material support in the form of military arms for use in the war. He regretted this, but understood it, again because India was one of our brother nations in the important Commonwealth. He said that his government would not even make a formal verbal protest against our action. But he then stated that he did resent a pronouncement made a day or two earlier by our Secretary of State for Foreign Affairs in the British Parliament. The Minister had described the Chinese as "the aggressors" in the war, declaring that the disputed area where the shooting occurred was part of India. This was incorrect. The place was not a part of India; it was a part of China. Therefore India was the aggressor.

I replied that I deeply appreciated his understanding of our British support for India as one of our partners in the Commonwealth. This was a noble expression of his friendly attitude towards the Commonwealth. Nonetheless I disagreed with what he had just said on the question of aggression. In my opinion our Minister was right to charge the Chinese with that wrongful act, because the areas in dispute had become parts of India long ago as a result of understandings reached between the British and the then Tibetan authorities. I acknowledged that the Chinese government of that time had refrained from recognizing the agreements, but I emphasized that they had been accepted by other nations. Indeed, I stated that they were shown as parts of India on maps in atlases published in many countries round the Earth.

With a smile Zhou remarked that he was delighted that a matter had arisen on which we could engage in keen controversy – which we then proceeded to do for quite a while. I need not go into details here about our arguments and counter-arguments. Zhou told me that during his talks with Nehru through the last several years, and also in exchanges of official letters with him, he had indicated that the Chinese government were willing to negotiate an agreement with the Indian government which recognized the entire region south of the MacMahon Line as a part of India, if the Indians would accept that Aksayqin was a part of China. He commented to me that Aksayqin was in fact a useless uninhabited area so far as India was concerned, whereas its space was important for China as an area of communication, transport and trade between two otherwise separated Chinese provinces.

He then said that this was the only subject that Nehru had always refused to discuss with him. The Indian leader kept asserting that both regions were inalienable parts of India. Zhou said to me that the Chinese had stayed patient about the problem, hoping for a peaceful settlement of it sooner or later by negotiations. Then the latest unfortunate shooting incident occurred between Chinese and Indian soldiers, with the consequent outbreak of fighting. In the opinion of the Chinese this was a case of them being attacked and having to counter-attack.

Zhou said that he and his colleagues did not wish the fighting to extend, and that they were proposing that delegations of the two governments should meet round a conference table to attempt to settle the matter friendlily. But he added that if the Indians persisted in provocative military action, the Chinese must respond. The Indians would be responsible for the consequences.

He then told me in confidence of the Chinese strategic plan if the fighting were to continue. He said that the war would be a very short one, stating that China's armed forces would quickly not only drive the weaker enemy wholly out of Aksayqin in the west but also advance a considerable distance south of the MacMahon Line in the eastern area of the disputed frontier. He asserted that they could continue advancing much further, but that the Chinese did not wish to acquire a single square inch of alleged Indian territory there. So when their conquering army had reached a certain point (which he indicated in broad terms to me) and had thus proved their ability to capture much wider regions, they would halt – and then voluntarily withdraw again to the north of the MacMahon Line. His government would repeat their readiness for peaceful, friendly negotiations on the whole problem. He hoped that this would persuade the Indians of the wisdom of the two sides sitting down together at a conference table and settling the frontier question in the sensible and mutually advantageous way that he suggested.

I expressed the view that the Chinese assault had aroused emotional Indian patriotic fervour to such a pitch that it would be impossible for Nehru, even if he now personally wished to do so, to engage in negotiations which would result in the cession of any part of India to China.

During the next three weeks military operations proceeded exactly as Zhou had foretold to me. Apparently confident of their ability to win the war, the Indians rejected the Chinese proposal that the two sides should meet for negotiations – and fighting broke out again. Chinese army units advanced everywhere to the areas which Zhou had indicated. They could have conquered much larger regions, but refrained. The government in Beijing then announced that it had no intention of retaining any territory which might properly be recognized as part of India, and the victorious Chinese troops promptly withdrew to the north of the old MacMahon Line everywhere else whilst remaining in occupation of Aksayqin. However, the Indian government still rejected the proposal for a peace conference which could consider a treaty settling the problem amicably in that manner.

The frontier between the two countries has in practice remained ever since as it got settled by the brief war.

Another war that was being fought alongside a different stretch of China's frontiers continued to be violently waged. It was the conflict in Vietnam between the Vietminh supported by Russian and Chinese military aid on one side and the South Vietnamese supported by American and other foreign military aid on the other.

Zhou Enlai, Chen Yi and I naturally discussed that potentially extremely explosive situation. Throughout the last thirteen years, ever since the Red Army completed its conquest of mainland China in 1949 and Mao set up a new government there which ruled the country with massive popular support, the Americans had refused to recognize that colossal, unchallengable fact. They adamantly declined to establish diplomatic or any other relations with the regime in Beijing. Instead they had shifted their Embassy to Taiwan (as Formosa came to be called) and continued to regard Chiang Kai-shek's administration there as the government of China – as if the huge mainland had disappeared from the face of the Earth and that small island was China. This was because of the continuing near-fanatical anti-Communist sentiments of not only a great majority of the American people but also some of the ruling authorities in

Boats moored in the sea off Xianggang

Washington. Moreover, it was in spite of the fact that they did recognize the Communist governments in Russia and some other lands.

Zhou Enlai and Chen Yi expressed to me their deep suspicion about the Americans' intentions regarding China. They believed that the leaders of that super-power perhaps planned to launch a military attack against it if (and when, as the Americans confidently expected) the Vietminh forces were defeated in the current Vietnamese war. The Americans could then acquire military bases in North Vietnam close beside China's frontier, and could use them for an all-out assault on Communist China. This would be in support of the allegedly legitimate Kuomintang government of China, whose army from Taiwan would nominally lead the attack by launching an invasion of the mainland. The aim would be to restore Chiang Kai-shek and his clique to power in Beijing.

The two Ministers explained that this was the only reason why the Chinese government were giving considerable military aid to the Vietminh fighting forces. It was for the defence of China itself. At the same time they said that they were not unduly apprehensive about an American assault because they expected that the Vietminh would eventually defeat the South Vietnamese, and so force the Americans to withdraw from Vietnam.

I tried to persuade them that the Americans now harboured no such intention against China. I argued that the Ministers' fear might well have been justified during the years when Foster Dulles was the Secretary of State in Washington, but that since his departure from the scene and the installation of the new government under President Kennedy any such plan had been abandoned. Indeed, I said that the Americans were now using their influence with Chiang Kai-shek to discourage him from making any unprovoked attack against the mainland. And I reminded them of the friendly attitude that the leader of the American delegation at the Geneva Conference on Laos, sagacious Averell Harriman, had shown towards Chen Yi and the Chinese delegation.

My companions had distinctly appreciated Harriman's personal relationship with them; but they remarked that in some ways the outlook of other Washington authorities seemed to have hardened further towards China since the conference. And they recalled that during the Korean War of some years earlier the American troops under General MacArthur's command had sought with their South Korean allies to defeat the North Korean army completely, advance to the Chinese frontier and (the Chinese suspected) invade part of China itself. It was to check that possible plan that the Chinese had then given military aid to the North Koreans, as they were now doing to the Vietminh.

The two Ministers expressed a hope that I was right in my belief of a changed American attitude, but repeated that they themselves were not convinced that this had yet happened. In support of their suspicion they pointed out that two-thirds of China was surrounded by military bases leased to the Americans by various countries allied to them, from Pakistan in the west to Vietnam, Thailand and the Philippine Islands in the south, and to Taiwan, South Korea and Japan in the east. They asserted that American propaganda in those countries sought to make them hostile to China. And they added that the Americans were now starting to give considerable aid to India in its military contest against China.

Nothing that I could say would remove from their minds their suspicion of a lingering American hostility towards China. At the same time Zhou expressed regret about the bad relations between America and China. He wished that they could become quite friendly, because the United States was one of the economically very sophisticated developed nations from which the Chinese could learn valuable lessons about how to organize as competently as possible in up-to-date technological ways the modernization of their own national economy. In particular the Americans could provide them with information and materials regarding the mechanization of their pre-eminently important agriculture.

The Ministers emphasized that the Chinese felt no prejudice against the American people, only against their government. They felt some respect for the Americans in general, and in particular were very grateful to the American author Edgar Snow for his sympathetic writings about their Communist Revolution in his book *Red Star Over China* and later journalistic articles.

At that time relations between China and several countries in South East Asia were uneasy. This was not so in the cases of Burma, Cambodia, Indonesia and now also, as a result of the Geneva Conference, Laos, all of which were non-aligned between the two super-powers at loggerheads in the "cold war". But Thailand and the Philippines were not only allies of the United States of America in that conflict, leasing military, air and in the latter case naval bases to the Americans; they also maintained diplomatic missions with Chiang Kai-shek's administration in Taiwan in opposition to Mao Zedong's government in Beijing. And although Malaya had established no such diplomatic association with Taiwan, it still refrained from recognizing the government in mainland China. Like Thailand and the Philippines, it was pro-Western and anti-Communist in its international outlook, as were also the still partly British ruled colonies of Singapore, North Borneo and Sarawak and the Protected State of Brunei.

One reason for this situation was that in several of the South East Asian lands, such as Malaya, where local Communist insurgents had through recent years been waging guerrilla wars against their popularly supported governments those rebels had received help from external Communist nations, including China. In my talks with Zhou Enlai and Chen Yi I commented that Beijing's support for those rebels made it impossible for friendly, good-neighbourly relations to grow between the countries concerned and China. This seemed to me a great pity from the point of view of developing peaceful co-existence widely through the Far East. I told the Ministers that in the conduct of my earlier official duties in the region I had advocated the establishment of a completely non-aligned South East Asia, whose governments and peoples could therefore be free to devote themselves to improving the economic and social well-being of their mostly newly independent nations. I had suggested that an international treaty should be negotiated between all the South East Asian governments themselves and the governments of the major external powers concerned, to achieve that aim. In it the South East Asian nations would agree to adopt policies of non-interference in each others' internal affairs, neutrality in the international "cold war", and the establishment of diplomatic relations with both sides in the conflict, whilst the United States of America, Russia, China, France and Britain would also undertake not to interfere at all in the internal political affairs of any of those lands, would give diplomatic recognition to their established governments, and would offer them financial and technical aid in their countries' economic development.

I remarked to the two Chinese Ministers that their government's support for Communist rebels in other lands was surely a breach of one of the Five Principles of Peaceful Co-existence, which declared that no government of a country should interfere in the internal affairs of another country.

They agreed that active aid to such rebels would be contrary to that principle; but they asserted that, although they naturally sympathized with the aspirations of the Communist insurgents concerned, their government had not given them any military or other material aid except in the case of the Vietminh guerrillas for the reason which I have already reported. They said that it had only given the others moral support in the form of broadcast commentaries on their radio and in other propagandist publications.

Zhou stated his belief that the peoples in each and every country in South East Asia should be free to choose whatever form of political government and national society they themselves wished. And he commented that he strongly favoured the idea of them all being non-aligned in the "cold war". Moreover, in that connection he added that he fully understood that some of the newly independent nations in South East Asia would wish to retain agreements for military co-operation between themselves and whichever of the European powers had previously been their Imperial ruler, such as those which already existed in the cases of Cambodia with France and of Malaya with Britain. The Chinese felt no objection to these because they were wholly defence agreements, for the protection of the small new nations against possible foreign attack. They were not designed to enable offensive action to be launched against some other nation, as the military alliances between Thailand and the Philippines on one hand and the United States of America on the other were. A principal purpose of those latter alliances was to help the Americans to make armed attacks against other countries such as Vietnam – and perhaps in due course China.

Zhou Enlai's and Chen Yi's attitude was of course consistent with the Chinese authorities' desire that their nation should be left in peace for many decades to come so that its government and population could concentrate their energies on the immense task of the massive modernization of their own People's Republic. At the same time I recognized that there was another reason why the Communist leaders in Beijing felt content to live for the present in peaceful co-existence with other nations practising different ideological systems. They believed that socialist revolutions were on the way throughout the world. In their judgement capitalist society was steadily disintegrating; it would in due course collapse everywhere, and be replaced by socialist, and indeed Communist, systems. According to their Marxist philosophy that prospect lay in the logic of history.

Zhou Enlai expressed the opinion that in any case Revolution cannot be imported by the people of one country into another. It can only be successfully achieved when a country's own population, roused by popular native leaders, themselves spontaneously decide to overthrow their reactionary rulers. Zhou felt that the prospective change was now brewing in parts of South East Asia, parts of Africa and parts of South America, and that in the foreseeable future it would spread steadily everywhere else.

The Ministers questioned me and I questioned them about various other aspects of international affairs. At one point in our talks about the changing scene round the Earth I asked the Ministers what was their attitude towards Hong Kong. They answered that I could assure the government in London that the Chinese authorities were in no hurry for any change in Hong Kong's position as a British colony. The island's continuation in that form for at least a considerable time to come suited the Chinese as well as us Britons. For instance, the facilities provided in that prosperous commercial seaport for China's trading with various overseas countries gained them foreign currencies which enabled them to keep increasing that trade in ways valuable to their Republic's economic development. Zhou gave me a clear impression that the situation could remain unaltered until 1997, when the lease by China to Britain of the mainland Kowloon territory now associated with Hong Kong island would lapse, and the matter must be re-examined. What should happen after that would depend on events in the meantime.

He emphasized that the situation regarding Taiwan island was entirely different. In the eyes of Mao Zedong's government – as indeed in those of Chiang Kai-shek and his colleagues – Taiwan was an integral, inseparable part of China, and nothing could alter that fact. Nevertheless Zhou Enlai and Chen Yi told me that the leaders in Beijing had no intention of taking the island by armed force – unless military provocation by some alien power such as America or Japan allied with Chiang Kai-shek's regime compelled them to act in that way. They were willing to be patient about Taiwan, for they believed that a majority of the people there were in favour of their island being part of China, and that after Chiang's death his successors might well spontaneously choose to reunite it with China under the present Beijing government. They were ready to wait for many years for that peaceful reunion.

One of the British government's acts about which the Ministers expressed appreciation was its support of resolutions introduced in the United Nations Assembly proposing that China should be elected a member of that Organization, contrary to the attitude of the American and many other delegations there who always succeeded in defeating those resolutions. At the same time they strongly criticized our British suggestion that Taiwan should continue to be a separate member of the U.N.O. after China's admission.

Those were the days when the extraordinary situation still persisted in which most of the nations round the world sought to ignore the existence of approximately 800,000,000 Chinese people – as if about a quarter of the Earth's contemporary human population had never been born!

6 The Cultural Revolution

NATIONAL ECONOMIC AND SOCIAL PROGRESS IN CHINA CONTINUED UNINTERRUPTED FOR a few years after 1962. Then the next crisis hit the state. It was the Cultural Revolution launched by Mao Zedong in 1966 and fully maintained for the next few years. People outside China were at a loss to understand why that turbulent, and at one time almost disastrous, eruption was sparked off. Many were inclined to suppose that it revealed a streak of megalomania in Mao, or perhaps even a touch of madness alongside genius starting to afflict him in his old age.

In 1968 I received an authoritative account of its true explanation and purpose from an eminent Head of Government of a newly emerging nation on another continent who, although not himself a Communist, felt sympathetic towards the new China. Worried by confusing reports, some good and some bad, of happenings there, he went to Beijing to learn at first-hand from the Chinese leaders themselves what was going on, and why.

Mao explained to him that the Chinese Revolution, like most other Revolutions in history, had been initiated by a small intellectual minority in the population. In the case of contemporary China that minority understood its Marxist–Leninist purpose, and as long as they retained supreme authority in the government the Revolution would move forward in proper directions. But (Mao continued) in every Revolution its creators' ideas were less understood by their successors; and indeed many of those new leaders were not inspired by the same principles. They tended to cast aside the aim of improving life for their fellow men, and to exploit governmental power to further their own selfish personal interests. So a return to reactionary policies began. This had occurred in France under Napoleon, in Russia under Kruschev – and it was now threatening to occur in China. Many bureaucrats in the central government in Beijing, in the various provincial capitals and at every level of local administration

79

were pursuing self-interest by starting to initiate policies which would push China off the road to socialism and lead it back to a capitalist road. If they got their way, the Revolution would collapse.

Mao had therefore insisted that steps should be taken to stop this from happening. What steps? In his view the Revolution could only be saved by teaching the masses of the people its purpose, so that they would keep sharp eyes on the party leaders, throw out of office those who held "revisionist" notions, and ensure that the correct Communist impetus of the Revolution was maintained. In fact the whole population must be turned into Revolutionaries enthused by the same ideology as moved the original intellectual minority. They would thus become the guardians of the Revolution.

Mao recognized that this could not be achieved very swiftly. It was impossible to educate 800,000,000 people all at once in the Marxist–Leninist philosophy as adapted by himself to suit Chinese conditions. The method of procedure must be to teach the doctrine to a succession of selected sections of the population, one after the other. He and his colleagues decided that the first section should be the armed forces – the troops in the People's Liberation Army who held the guns which had enabled the Communist Party to gain and maintain its victory. The famous *Little Red Book* of *Quotations from Chairman Mao Tse-tung* was therefore produced to indoctrinate them with his teachings. Its study became a part of every soldier's military training.

When their learning was completed Mao and his supporters decided that the next section to be taught must be the members of the young, rising generation – those important youths who would become the rulers of China tomorrow, and whose support was therefore vital if the Revolution was to be continuously maintained. So first the university students, then the middle school youngsters, and afterwards all the primary school children in the urban area were instructed by the *Little Red Book* in the Thoughts of Mao. By the time that this job was finished in late 1966 some 100,000,000 Chinese were his well-tutored, zealous disciples.

Then the astonishing act of closing all the universities and schools in the urban centres was taken, at his command. A complete stoppage of the young people's scholastic education there was enforced. For the next period ahead those youngsters' education was to consist of learning how to conduct a Revolution in practice. For this purpose many of them were mobilized into companies of Red Guards. They were told to go into the streets, factories and offices to spread the political progaganda in which they had been indoctrinated, to recruit allies among the workers, and to see that "revisionists", "capitalist roaders" and other such traitors were ousted from the local executive bodies in all the organizations everywhere and that proper revolutionaries took their places.

Mao told my informant that such a refreshment of the Revolution should take place periodically, probably at intervals of approximately every ten years.

Much could be written about the events which as a consequence rocked China during the next few years. For long the youngsters were given a free hand to do whatever they thought necessary to ensure the persistent growth of a truly Communist state. My informant told me that he learned that the Army was ordered not to interfere with them, but to give them wholehearted support. Even if a boy or a girl in excess of zeal slapped a soldier on the face, the latter must not strike back! And in numerous places the Red Guards or other groups of agitators ran amok, using awful violence. The forceful take-over for several days of the Ministry of Foreign Affairs in Beijing, and the burning of the British Diplomatic Mission's building there were examples of this.

Gradually the committees running provinces, municipalities, factories and other institutions throughout the urban areas got purged of alleged "reactionaries". But in the process heated arguments often broke out between opposing factions among cadres and workers, causing fisticuff fights. In numerous workshops partial or entire walk-outs occurred – and a very serious decline in industrial production resulted. Indeed, in some areas government itself almost broke down, and chaos threatened.

Then the Army was ordered to intervene, to uphold law and order. Their weapons for doing this were not to be guns, but copies of the *Little Red Book*. They were to enter factories and other institutions wherever quarrellings persisted, talk firmly to the rival factions, and reconcile them by compelling them to co-operate on the basis of Mao's Thoughts. Later they were to conduct a similar education campaign about his Thoughts throughout all the communes. Under their dedicated leadership new Revolutionary Committees – composed partly of old, experienced local leaders whose ideological views were above reproach, and partly of ardent new ones – gradually assumed control in every organization. By the time that my friend visited Beijing order was already restored almost, though not yet quite, everywhere throughout the country.

Children sketching in the Square of Heavenly Peace, Beijing

He told me that Zhou Enlai, Lin Biao (Lin Piao) and other important leaders whom he met looked thin, exhausted and ill. By contrast Mao Zedong appeared very hale and hearty. He had sparked off the Cultural Revolution, and then sat back in his chair reading books, writing more of his thoughts – and leaving those colleagues to strive in practice day by day, month after month, and indeed through years to guide it safely along its dangerous path. This was a difficult, sometimes nearly impossible task which taxed their energies and abilities almost beyond endurance. But in the end they succeeded in preventing the nation from collapsing chaotically – and themselves survived.

Premier Zhou Enlai was the principal person who guided events back from irresponsible political extremism to responsible administration. In the process the wilder young Red Guards whose undisciplined actions threatened to spread anarchy were deprived of their influential positions and sent instead to do helpful agricultural or other labour in newly developing distant areas of the country. But in the meantime many truly responsible individuals had become political casualties. During the worst period of upheavals, when ultra-leftist zealots had gained virtual control of some departments of government, numerous capable civil servants and other experienced persons who disagreed with their outlooks were dismissed from their offices. A typical example was Deng Xiaoping (Teng Hsiao-ping), who for some time had been the able and sincere but anti-extremist Secretary-General of the Communist Party. He was ejected from that important post, and in effect sent into exile.

The most eminent of those exiles was Liu Shaoqi (Liu Shao-chi), who had for some time been the Chairman of the People's Republic of China, the formal Head of State. A very able administrator, for practical reasons he had opposed what he regarded as the too hasty introduction of some socialist plans for national economic progress. This brought him into political conflict with Mao Zedong and other ultra-leftists. The Cultural Revolution was in fact not only an attempt by Mao to achieve his avowed aim of "purifying the Revolution" but also a power struggle in which he sought to get rid of some of his critics. Liu was denounced by Mao's extremist supporters as "a capitalist roader"; and he was expelled from power.

At one time Mao himself made a self-criticism, admitting to some high officials that at one point during the Cultural Revolution things got badly out of hand, going considerably beyond his original intentions.

7 China Moves Onward

I NEXT RETURNED TO CHINA IN 1971, AGAIN AS A GUEST OF ITS GOVERNMENT INVITED BY Zhou Enlai. During a month I journeyed widely through ten varied regions in which I visited fifty different industrial, agricultural, educational, cultural and other establishments, talking with the people and viewing current conditions. The central government was strong, all the provincial administrations were loyal to it, the "purged" Communist Party had been reconstructed at all levels, and under its policy-making direction the recently established Revolutionary Committees ran all the factories, communes and local institutions. Peaceful law and order prevailed, and the people appeared to feel united. Some tensions remained among certain members of the inner circle of top rulers, but they did not disturb that general state of affairs.

The sense of unity which bound the people together was partly due to the composition of the Revolutionary Committees. Their members were chosen to represent two different three-way groupings. The first was the army (or in some cases the militia), the cadres and the workers in the urban areas or the peasants in the rural areas; and the second was the old generation, the middle-aged people and the young. It was pleasant to see how amicably all those groups co-operated with one another.

Another feature of the Revolutionary Committees illustrated the purpose of the Cultural Revolution. The chairman of each committee everywhere was a Red Army soldier or an official who was a member of the Communist Party. In every factory, for instance, its highly experienced and knowledgeable Managing Director did not preside over the committee's discussions. He was a member of the team, but his economic expertise was regarded as less important than the political judgement of a local Communist leader in settling policies for running the industrial works. The denigration of the "national capitalists" was emphasized in another way too. They were deprived without any compensation of all their remaining financial investments in their previously owned factories, and also of some of their other property such as large family houses.

During my travels I observed many of the results of the recent episode. I can touch only briefly on a few of them here. Undoubtedly during its most tumultuous period industrial production in some workshops had stopped altogether for a while, and in many others it seriously declined. So the rate of national economic advance was not merely slowed, but here and there thrown into reverse. Now, late in 1971, I was told that it was starting to go full-steam ahead again. This was partly because Zhou Enlai and the supporters of his sagacious policies had gradually succeeded in reinstating many, though very far from all, of the previously expelled experienced and able officials in fresh government posts. One of these was Deng Xiaoping, whom Zhou appointed as a Vice-Premier. Indeed, Zhou appeared to be grooming him to become in due course his own possible successor as Prime Minister.

Another important reason for the gradually resuming progress was that, in contrast to the serious setbacks in various urban areas, agricultural progress had suffered less troubles, and had continued more or less steadily throughout the Cultural Revolution. Although some of the unfortunate policies being pursued were extended, with partially ill effects, into the communes' affairs, the upheaval's most vicious aspects hardly intruded into the countrysides. Political changes there – such as the appointments of the Revolutionary Committees in the communes – were achieved more peacefully. Moreover, because the multitude of new irrigation, afforestation, electric power and other schemes were making every region less liable to the damages previously wrought by droughts, floods and typhoons, a continuous succession of good harvests had blessed the land throughout the last ten years.

I saw evidence of some other important economic innovations which had occurred during that decade. For instance, whereas coal had previously been produced only in the north and was transported to the south for use there, and rice used to be grown only in the south and had to be transported for eating in the north, both north and south now produced considerable quantities of those two commodities. Again, contrary to the reckoning of earlier geologists who asserted that oil could not exist in workable quantities anywhere in China, rich deposits of it had been discovered in various regions; and it was now being extracted on a scale which could grow steadily until the Chinese became independent of foreign imports of oil. In addition several other crucially important, hitherto undetected or neglected minerals were also being mined, and could help to make China more and more self-reliant. And able Chinese scientists were starting China along the road to becoming a nuclear power, with help from visiting American-trained Chinese who lived in America.

Incidentally, during 1970 more than 240 million tons of grain had been produced, a figure indicating that the reckoning by Zhou Enlai and Chen Yi eight years earlier that it would take about ten years to expand agriculture in China to a point where it supplied sufficient of the basic food requirements of the whole population was near the mark. In 1970 the Chinese had bought only a little more than $2\frac{1}{2}$ million tons of grain from overseas – an infinitesimal quantity in relation to the nation's total consumption. Moreover, at least that amount was probably put into reserve that year, in accordance with the government's policy of storing grain as an insurance against any possible disasters. In fact by then altogether 40 million tons were in storage.

During my enquiries that year I found that the rates of pay for industrial workers had scarcely changed since 1962. Except for slight rises in a comparatively few cases,

Tricycles used to carry the sick as well as everyday commodities

they remained just about the same. A representative example was the wages paid in a medium-sized factory which I visited in Nanjing. Although rates were rather lower in certain different establishments like handicraft workshops in the city, and were a bit higher in some others, these figures were similar to those that I was given in many other factories. The lowest grade of workers received 40 yuan a month, those in the highest grade received 108 yuan, and the average wage of the workers in all the grades amounted to 60 yuan. The lowest grade of technicians received 46 yuan a month, and the highest (the chief engineer) got 180 yuan. Cadres received sums of between 40 and 146 yuan, according to their grades.

One yuan was worth approximately 17 English pence, which made those incomes seem to a Westerner very small, since on that reckoning a lowest grade worker earned the equivalent of less than £7 a month. But what mattered, of course, was the prices which he or she had to pay for necessities and other goods. In the cases of the averagely representative group of individuals which I am quoting, important items worked out as follows. Rent for a single-room flat was 2 yuan and 40 cents a month, for a two-roomed flat 4 yuan, and for a three-roomed flat 7.80 yuan, all with running water, central heating and electricity supplied free. The occupants shared a kitchen and toilet with other tenants for no extra charge. Food cost between 12 and 15 yuan per month for each individual eating three meals a day. Daily care of the workers' children in a factory's nursery cost them nothing, and the education of their youngsters in primary and middle schools cost 2 yuan a year, including the supply of textbooks. Medical treatment in clinics and hospitals was free for the workers themselves, whilst they paid half the costs for their dependents, the other half being provided by the factory.

Since a husband and his wife nearly always both worked, their family income was more or less doubled, and adult children who lived with them also contributed to the sum. They all had complete security in jobs, for one of the astonishing things I found in China in 1971 was that there was no unemployment. Male workers usually retired at the age of 60, and women at 55, with pensions amounting to about 70% of their last rate of pay.

I was told in another typical factory that the total cost of the necessities of life for an average-paid married couple without children was such that they could spend almost 50% of their pay on other things. Pairs with two youngsters could save a little for such spending. If they wished to invest some of it, every factory had its savings bank where money could be deposited with a modest rate of interest paid per year. And the qualities and varieties as well as the quantities of consumer goods which could be brought in shops had increased very considerably since I had toured those shops in 1962 – almost all of the goods having been made in China itself. Their costs were extremely low compared with those customary outside China. Moreover, the prices for essential foodstuffs had been compulsorily stabilized by the government. Grain was still rationed because of the policy of keeping vast amounts of it in storage, but the rationing of many other types of food which had existed in 1962 had now been abolished. These had become in plentiful supply. A ration per person of cotton cloth for suits and dresses did continue, but its length had been somewhat increased. Favourite items of purchase by the workers in towns and the peasants in the country-sides, after they had acquired all the household goods that they needed, were sewing-machines, bicycles, transistor radios (although progressively more radio equipment was being provided free in tenement flats in urban areas and in cottages in communes), clocks, wrist-watches, and toys for the children. The production of some of these articles was not keeping up with the growing demand, and for them a purchaser had to acquire a coupon. The prices of certain goods had been reduced everywhere, medicines in particular being much cheaper. In some parts of the country the prices of some other wares were lower than during my previous visit, whilst in other instances the prices were about the same although the qualities of the wares had improved. So on the whole the standard of living of the people had risen a little bit through recent years.

I observed a typical example of the improvement in the qualities of goods being made in China when I went to a factory in Shanghai where wrist-watches were being manufactured. Through the years their producers had been learning to construct them from models imported from Switzerland. I was told two interesting things regarding them. First, the Chinese watchmakers were still only gradually acquiring perfect skills in their elaborate construction. In 1958 the watches which they contrived had lost $1\frac{1}{2}$ minutes of time during every 24 hours, and so had to be adjusted accordingly each day. By 1960 they were losing only 1 minute in every 24 hours; and now, in 1971, the loss had been reduced to 25 seconds. Their makers hoped to eliminate that brief defect in the very near future.

The manager of the factory told me the second interesting thing that I learned. He said that he was receiving many letters of complaint from women purchasers of the watches. Their epistles protested that none of the five different types of watches being produced were "pretty" enough for feminine use. They were, for instance, too large – the same size as the ones being worn by their heftier menfolk. Could the factory please start to create much smaller watches for wearing on women's wrists? This was a pleasing sign of the growing desire of the maidens and dames for prettier feminine articles of wear.

In every factory that I visited I observed that the ordinary workers themselves were invited to take a part in devising progressive improvements in the capacity of its machinery to produce the sort of goods needed in current Chinese circumstances. The authorities did this partly to encourage goodwill by them in implementing the policy of industrial development, and partly because they recognized that the practical intelligence of those workers could in any case be of positive inventive assistance to the experts in that field of endeavour. In every factory a Technical Innovation Group therefore existed, composed of cadres, technicians and workers who met periodically to discuss together the problems of mechanical improvements.

This was one element in a touch of democracy which was practised in the people's daily working activities. In the workshops, for instance, boards were hung on walls where there were not only notices of information or instructions by the management but also written expressions of opinion about this or that relevant subject by the workers themselves. It stimulated constructive discussions on how their co-operative aims could most effectively be achieved.

Having written all the information above I must add that although the people's standard of living was far higher than the members of the old and middle-aged generations who remembered conditions before 1949 had then ever dreamed to be possible, it was still very modest indeed compared with that of working people in economically developed countries. The homes of the Chinese were very simply

Picking and drying green tea in Hangzhou

furnished, their clothing was limited though adequate, and their comforts were relatively few. But other new amenities which they had never enjoyed before were now available to them at little or no cost, such as buses for transport, cinemas and theatres for entertainment, sports grounds for recreations, and public parks for relaxation on off-days.

One got a vivid impression of the very early stage of growth towards an affluent society which existed by watching street scenes in the cities and large towns. Surprisingly few motor-cars appeared. No individual could afford to own one. Even the salaries of high-up government Ministers were too low for them to possess such a luxury. Of course, state-owned cars were available to take them on official journeys, as well as for other public purposes like driving eminent foreign guests around. Bicycles – pedal bicycles, not motor bikes – were the means of transport for countless people, and although their numbers had already been quite considerable in 1962 they had multiplied enormously since then. At hours when factory hands were going to or from work streams of them sped along the streets. For those who were not yet able to buy a bike buses were available, and these too had vastly increased in numbers between 1962 and 1971. Again, they had all been produced in factories in China.

Heavy motor vehicles were becoming more and more in evidence. Yet the supply of them was still clearly very inadequate, for in many places innumerable much smaller, more primitive means of transport continued to be used. Some were tricycles, tri-shaws and other suchlike carriers pedalled by old fellows who in character looked similar to, but in physical health stronger than, the rickshaw-pullers of bygone days. However, much commoner in most towns were carts. Some of these were drawn by horses, mules, donkeys or bullocks, or by teams of two, three or four of those beasts. But many others were carts dragged by human beings, sometimes by their tugging hands and at other times by ropes stretched like reins round their shoulders. Those folks-of-burden were men, women and children alike. Often the load on a cart was very heavy, and the pullers bore a much greater strain than they should have done. Occasionally among the baggage being lugged along was an old man or woman or some other passenger lolling aboard regardless of the extra labour involved for the tugger.

In the rural countrysides a similar mixture of simple means of transport meandered along the roads, with a much smaller proportion of motor vehicles, distinctly fewer (though increasingly plentiful) bicycles, and a higher proportion of animal or human-drawn carts. In the southern provinces the population of water-buffaloes continued to be large, and they wandered around as nonchalantly as their forebears had done for centuries, indifferent to the more sophisticated mechanical types of conveyance which now and then trundled past them, and which would have astonished their ancestors. More customary for them was another means of freight transport which remained very common – the numerous peasants trotting along the highways and byways carrying lengthy shoulder-poles with heavily laden baskets dangling from each end.

Another mark of the simplicity of life in contemporary China was the uniform style of clothing which almost all the people wore, whether they were at work or at play. Men and women alike – workers, peasants, cadres, academics, government ministers and others – usually sported dark blue or grey jackets and trousers. It was true that the quality of the cloth was finer in the cases of government officials and some other individuals, but the type of the garments was standardized. Only small children, and schoolboys and schoolgirls on special ceremonial occasions, were now starting to stroll around in gaily coloured garments. No one wore rags, as so many of them did twenty-three years ago. They all had an adequate supply of comfortable clothing, but it was plain and often rather drab.

Incidentally, one of my regrets about the state of affairs in China in 1962 which I had mentioned to Zhou Enlai when he then asked me for my criticisms concerned this matter of dress. I expressed great sorrow at the complete disappearance of, for instance, the beautifully graceful, decorative cheongsams which used to be the traditional daily attire of ladies throughout the country, and which still continued to be the everyday costume worn by young and older Chinese women in South East Asia and other lands elsewhere.

Zhou agreed with my regret, and said that he looked forward to the time when more

Above : Malcolm MacDonald making one of many visits to industrial plants

Below : A worker adjusts her machine in Shanghai No. 2 Machine Tool Factory

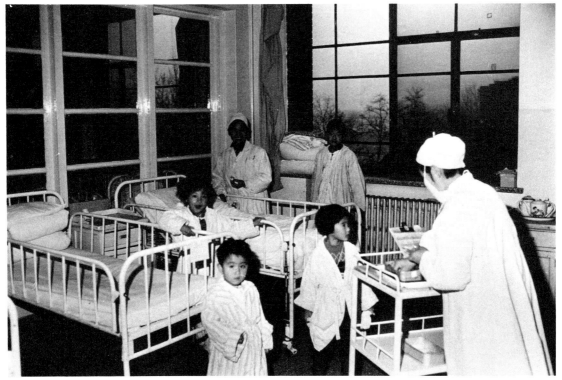

Above: Children seem happy and relaxed even at medicine time in Beijing's Childrens' Hospital

Below: Herbal medicines in a Guangzhou Commune pharmacy

attractive clothing could be worn by the women, and also the men, outside their working hours. But he commented that the production of such garments had a low priority in the list of objects which must be produced in developing China. The urgent need for agricultural and industrial advance on a huge scale, and for steady increases in the supplies of absolute necessities and simple conveniences for use by all the large population meant that the output of multitudes of various sorts of tools, machinery, vehicles, elementary household furnishings, school equipments, hospital instruments and so on must have higher places in the production programmes. In addition the making of adequate quantities of plain working clothing must also have precedence over gay dresses, jackets, jerseys and other such elaborate wear. But Zhou promised that when I returned to China on one of my visits several years later I would see the people starting to wear such garments, including (he hoped) decorative cheongsams on the women.

His prophecy was now, in 1971, beginning to come true. In cloth-making workshops I saw charming red and yellow as well as grey and blue fabrics being produced for females' work-time garments. And I learned that when their day's work was done, in their homes in the evenings, some women were starting to put on pretty dresses. But no cheongsams were yet in sight.

Still in the streets an occasional old crone hobbling along on her miniature bound feet was a relic of the pre-Revolutionary, almost dead past. I also heard an echo of that past in a silk-thread factory in Wuxi (Wuhsi). A woman member of its Revolutionary Committee was introduced to me as a "veteran worker". The description astonished me because she looked so young. On enquiry I learned that she was indeed only 34 years old, but that she had toiled in the mill for twenty-six years, having begun to do so as an 8-years-old child in 1945. And about 80% of her many hundreds of contemporaries tending its machines were similar "veterans".

One question that then arose was: could the people's standard of living be raised substantially further in the near future? In spite of the partial setback during the Cultural Revolution the national wealth had increased so enormously over the last decade that this could be done – if the authorities felt it wise to allocate a larger proportion of the state's huge financial profits from industrial and agricultural production to extra pay for workers and peasants instead of to investment in further capital expansion. During the last several years they had judged that this would be imprudent; the continuous economic growth required by the nation if it was to become reasonably soon a highly developed state was so colossal that it needed non-stop vast investments, and would probably continue to do so for the next two or three decades. The leaders had to bear in mind that even a slight rise in pay for individuals would cost a gigantic sum because they numbered several hundreds of millions of people.

Another factor was that those leaders considered it better to spend large sums of money on expanding public welfare services – like those provided in hospitals, health clinics, kindergartens, schools, sports stadiums, recreation centres and other such institutions – for everyone's free use everywhere, than to hand it out in extra wages. Nevertheless, during my inspection tours of industries and in talks with authorities in Beijing I gained an impression that they were contemplating the possibility of a rise in pay for the lowest one, two or three grades of workers – but not for the higher grades – in the foreseeable future as the next step towards achieving their goal of a much more egalitarian, as well as better, way of life for the multitudes.

Opposite : Training future soldiers at the Shanghai Children's Palace
Above : Physical training on Sheng Commune, outside Beijing
Academic work on display at Changsha Middle School, Hunan

Other interesting developments which had occurred in recent years concerned the practice of health care and medical treatment. Soon after 1949 thousands of health clinics were established, and the number of hospitals was also very considerably increased everywhere throughout the country, to care for the physical and mental fitness of everyone in the population. And because of the shortage of professionally trained physicians and nurses tens of thousands of so-called "barefoot doctors", men and women alike, were given a short but very useful course of tuition in the simplest essential medical practices. In every village of every commune and every residential area of every factory they tended the sick on visits to their homes or in the local clinics.

Mao's government also urged that doctors who pursued ancient traditional Chinese "herbal" or other methods of healing and those who were educated as modern Western-style medical practitioners should co-operate together, exchanging knowledge about what was best in each of their customs, and combining the two in mutual collaboration whenever this could benefit ailing patients. So in every hospital there were groups of representatives of both types on its staff of physicians and surgeons.

I witnessed some results of this co-operation in the operating theatres of a hospital in Shanghai, where I watched three operations. The first was for the sterilization of a woman, the second to extract a cartilage from a youth's knee, and the third to remove a large chunk of the intestines from the stomach of an old man. All the horrid cuts involved were made by Western-trained surgeons, and throughout the process the patients stayed wide awake, smiling and occasionally chatting, because the sliced-up parts of their bodies were rendered numb by traditional acupuncture anaesthesia. I remember well the serene mood of the old man throughout his grim operation. He was a peasant who had been brought to the hospital from a remote rural area, and he realized that no such chance of healing would have been available to him a score of years earlier. When a considerable part of his interior had been successfully extracted and the surgeon was sewing-up the wound in his flesh, the removed intestines were carried past him in a large bowl. He glanced at it, chuckled and murmured, "Long live Chairman Mao!"

A Chinese friend who was a Western-trained doctor told me that she had watched an operation performed by similar methods on an aged woman suffering from a brain tumour. Whilst the surgeon's knife cut at part of her brain the old girl kept grinning. But at one moment she did complain that she felt a pain in her foot!

In Guangchou I saw another notable achievement of acupuncture anaesthesia. One of the new education services initiated by the Communist government after 1949 was the establishment of schools for deaf-and-dumb children in many parts of the country. At that time the pupils could only communicate extremely inadequately with their teachers and each other by expressive looks in their eyes and meaningful jerks of their hands, fingers and thumbs. In 1968, however, a doctor had discovered that acupuncture injections made periodically over months in certain parts of the youngsters' bodies could in many cases gradually give them hearing – and once their ears could listen to

Opposite: Looking down on Shanghai from the top of Shanghai Mansions. In the foreground is the old Garden Bridge which marked the boundary of the International Settlement and over which William MacQuitty passed in 1939 through the Japanese lines en route for England via the Trans-Siberian Railway

the sound of voices they also began to learn to talk. I visited one of the schools, and sat in a series of classrooms where the students had reached different stages of this process. In the equivalent of a sixth-form class, where the most advanced group of recent deaf-mutes had been receiving that treatment for over a year, they put on a performance of play-acting, singing and recitations for me, including slogans of thanks to Chairman Mao for giving them a new life. They all spoke extremely well.

Doctors were then trying to use acupuncture for curing deafness in older people, but so far without the success that had been achieved among many, though not all, of the children. I understand that their efforts in that field still continue to fail.

One of the significant results of the Cultural Revolution was a change in the system of education. Prior to it schooling for the masses of the young people – which before 1949 had scarcely existed for any except the children of upper class families – had expanded by leaps and bounds. Nursery schools were abundant for infants everywhere, primary schools had multiplied until more than 90% of all youngsters of that age group were said to study in their class-rooms, and middle school education was provided for a large proportion of the total population of teenagers. Moreover, very many of the illiterate older people in towns and villages alike had learned in adult evening classes to read and write.

As I have mentioned, during the Cultural Revolution many schools and universities were closed, and others suspended their classes for a while. The Cultural Revolution reforms which were introduced after their reopening affected primary school teaching to some extent, but were more radical regarding the middle schools and universities. In discussions on the subject some of the authorities explained to me that the changes were still "experimental", and that only after further practical experience would final decisions be taken about this or that aspect of them.

For the present, at least, the period of middle school education had been reduced from six to five years, and it might later be further reduced to four. This meant that pupils now left school at the age of 16, and might later do so at 15. The curriculum was also being considerably modified. For instance, classes for learning Marxist–Leninist ideology in general and the Thoughts of Mao in particular were being increased. At a typical school that I visited in Beijing they were the first class held for all the students every day, each lasting for 45 minutes. Scholastic subjects like mathematics were being made less theoretical and more practical, with quite frequent statistical references to such matters as China's economic development plans. Again, every middle school now had its own workshop for making or repairing types of industrial goods, and every pupil worked at its simple machines for one month each year. The purpose of this was to teach the youngsters that manual labour is honourable, as well as to train their hands in some of its techniques which might be necessary for their type of work after leaving school. In addition they spent another month every year doing farm labour in communes – as members of government departments, college professors, school teachers and other professional people also did. So all the students spent eight months doing scholastic work including Communist ideological lessons, one month learning industrial tasks, and another month gaining experience of practical agriculture. During their two months' holidays many of them went camping for a while in the countryside, where part of their time was devoted to militia-type physical training.

The number of technical and agricultural training schools for youngsters of middle school age was being increased. Another feature of the educational reforms was remarkable. With very rare exceptions no students now passed immediately from middle schools into universities. On the contrary, after leaving school they must do two or three years whole-time work as mechanics in factories, peasants in communes or soldiers in the army, or at different times in more than one of those capacities. Only after this could the allegedly best qualified of them become candidates for places in universities. Moreover, both in middle and higher education the examination system had been abolished. The boys and girls eventually chosen for admission to universities were selected not by their capacity to pass academic tests, but partly by the votes of their fellow labourers concerning their personal characters and general competence, and mostly by the judgement of the local Communist Party authorities regarding their ideological political rectitude. My informants emphasized that this meant that children of workers and peasants had as good a chance of selection as did the youngsters of cadres, soldiers, teachers or other intellectual persons. There was said to be no class discrimination either way.

The successful candidates thus entered universities or other institutions of higher learning at the age of 19 or 20. A further change was that all of their courses in those places were being reduced to three years instead of the often longer periods of earlier times. In addition almost all post-graduate studies were abolished. It was thought that the reductions in the lengths of both school and university education would make no difference to the knowledge and capacities of the ultimate graduates. Their work would be more streamlined, and the practical experiences of industrial, agricultural, technical and scientific matters which the comprehensive scheme – plus their tuition in the Marxist–Leninist–Maoist ideology – promoted would result in the youngsters becoming more useful citizens. After they completed their higher education they would mostly return to the urban or rural areas where they had previously lived and worked, to make their professional, technical or other contributions there.

I was told repeatedly that one purpose of all this was to break down the old divisions between urban and rural communities, between military and civilian personnel, and between workers, peasants, administrators, academics and other professional types. The government was striving to create a united classless society whose citizens were all equal comrades.

As I have already mentioned, some people (including Zhou Enlai, I must add) said to me that the changes were only at "an experimental stage". Their worth would be judged by the results, and further modifications in one way or another in the education policy might be introduced later. I felt instinctively that those individuals were very concerned about some of the consequences of the so-called reforms, such as the serious lowering of the academic standards of newly trained professional people which was evidently occurring.

The most significant result of the Cultural Revolution was the wholesale indoctrination in Mao's Thoughts which had been spread throughout the population. One of the striking facts about China when I travelled there in 1962 was that, although everyone

Overleaf: Beijing from the top of Coal Hill with the Imperial Palace in the foreground and the Gate of Heavenly Peace beyond

recited phrases of Communist slogans, only a tiny percentage of its citizens had any idea what Communism was all about, and the others were content to remain ignorant on the subject. They were neither pro-Communist nor anti-Communist. They realized that the government was doing a good job at improving their living conditions; and so they felt loyal to it. But they never gave any serious thought to the Thoughts of Mao.

Now that state of affairs had completely changed. As I have already mentioned, at the height – or the depth – of the Cultural Revolution, when the often vicious quarrellings between different factions caused unfortunate consequences in many places, the members of the People's Liberation Army were sent everywhere to end the troubles and restore co-operative unity throughout the population. Their principal weapon for achieving this was the *Little Red Book*. In the troubled urban areas and the peaceful rural regions alike they organized classes to teach the common people their Leader's Thoughts. So the gospel according to Chairman Mao got widely spread. And this sort of missionizing activity had been earnestly maintained by Communist Party members among the masses ever since. In every workshop of every factory, every village of every commune, every faculty of every university, and every unit of every other organization study groups met on several days each week to read, recite and discuss their great tutor's teachings. Countless thousands of such groups existed, each one of a manageable size consisting of anything between half-a-dozen and twenty to thirty individuals. In factories that I visited, for example, they met for an hour or two after working shifts on three, four or more days every week. Nor was the subject of their study necessarily confined to the *Little Red Book;* it often included other of Mao's writings, and sometimes extended to Marx's and Engels' *Communist Manifesto* and a few related works. Those publications could all be bought extremely cheaply in bookshops.

I felt very critical of one result of those exercises. For a Westerner used to free, controversial discussions on all sorts of human issues it was worrying to hear how the Communist phraseology got imbibed and then spouted over and over again by millions and millions of individuals in precisely the same jargon, with no apparent flicker of dissent. Almost every worker, peasant, student, intellectual and other character whom I met anywhere repeated Mao's socialist theories, anti-revisionist denunciations and other ideological notions in exactly the same words, sentences and indeed whole paragraphs. Nor was that all. Their friendly expressions of greetings to foreign visitors and their kindly phrases of thanks to them for amicable comments were reiterated in the same formulae by just about everyone I talked with – old and young, townees and rustics, northerners, southerners, easterners and westerners – almost as if I were listening to utterances by vast regiments of parrots.

I felt particularly uneasy when the reciters were children in primary or indeed even nursery schools. I hugely enjoyed watching theatrical performances by groups of Little Red Soldiers in concert halls. They were healthy, smiling, charming youngsters neatly dressed in colourful school costumes who sang, danced and acted with engaging competence. But their dialogues often contained slick Communist slogans. Such pronouncements could be tolerable when spoken by adult members of Revolutionary Committees, production teams, party forums and other groups who presumably more or less comprehended the meaning of what they were saying; but they became upsetting in the mouths of little toddlers who could have little or no such understanding. Yet perhaps I should have recalled that in my own childhood my classmates and I in our

Sorting cocoons and testing the silk in Wuxi Silk Factory

Above : Machines in the Wuxi Brocade Factory

Opposite top : Treatment by acupuncture and moxibustion for facial palsy at the Beijing Childrens Hospital and a deaf mute being treated by acupuncture at the Deaf and Dumb Children's Institute at Guangzhou where there have been good results from this method for curing deafness due to injury and damage

Opposite bottom : Barefoot doctors in a Guangzhou Farm Commune. They are the front line in the prevention of disease

kindergarten school, and all our contemporaries in other such establishments, were ordered to stand up like companies of infant soldiers each morning and sing:

> "Rule Britannia!
> Britannia, rule the waves.
> Britons never, never, never shall be slaves . . ."

In any case, having written all that I must add another of my strong impressions. In one respect the uniformly repetitive talk appeared very moving. I realized that among the multitude of adults and older teenagers the formulae were apparently not uttered artificially as recitations learned by heart for stage performances. They were spoken not simply from the heads but also the hearts of those humble folk, who repeated them with enthusiastically sincere conviction. They believed that Mao's Thoughts expressed the Truth, and their individual and collective conduct in everyday life was guided by it.

I should express another of my mixed, sometimes rather mutually conflicting reactions to what I saw and heard. I wondered whether the previously illiterate, usually poverty-stricken, oppressed and traditionally autocratically disciplined Chinese masses could have been aroused to their current revival as a potentially great nation by any other means than some such stupendous regimentation. It may have been the essential

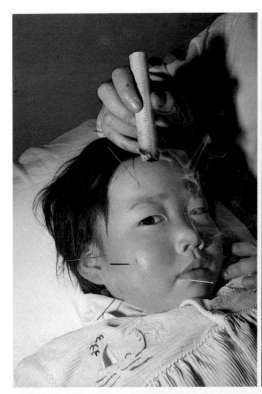
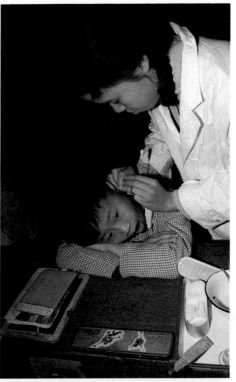

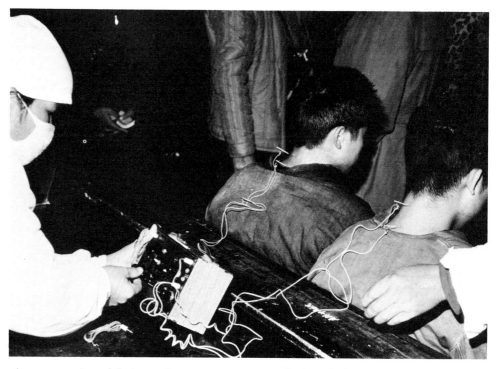

Acupuncture is used during major surgery as an anaesthetic and also in the treatment of psychiatric disorders in Hunan Psychiatric Hospital

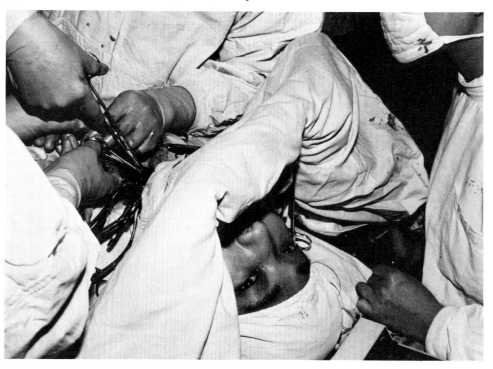

means of achieving the transition from national weakness back to national strength. Certainly, in spite of the criticisms of aspects of it which many may feel, it was doing tremendous good for the personal well-being of those now about 800,000,000 people.

That brings me to another significant point. The Thoughts of Mao which had been drilled into the minds of the multitudes did not consist only of a statement of Marxist–Leninist political philosophy as interpreted by him to suit Chinese conditions. Parts of them laid down the law about the ethical conduct which every individual should respect and practise. So they included what amounted to a moral code of proper personal behaviour. For example, they stated that no one should be inspired by selfish personal ambition; the motive of all action should not be self-advancement but service to one's fellow-men. For this reason nobody should harbour a desire for undue material gain as a reward for work, but should wish simply to be a helpful member of the community who received for his or her labour the same satisfaction of their needs as other people got. This was the explanation why hotel waiters and waitresses, railway porters and other assistants everywhere in China then refused to accept tips for anything that they did. Other exhortations in the *Little Red Book* were for hard work, initiative, frugality, modesty and various related virtues.

Some of the reforms which had been introduced into China soon after 1949 destroyed practices that had ruled Chinese society throughout centuries. One of the first of them was the elevation of women to a status of equality in principle with men. Thus males and females were given equal pay for equal work in industry, agriculture and every other field of activity. One consequence of this greater respect for the position of women was that expectant mothers who worked in factories were granted several weeks' maternity leave on full pay. And many women held quite high positions in the management of industries, communes and some other organizations in the country. Nevertheless, none of them yet held influential offices in the central government.

Another extremely important reform which established more equality between the members of the two sexes was that the right of a man to have more than one wife at a time, or to keep concubines, was abolished. From the moment when this law was enacted in May 1950 monogamy became the rule, although provision was made for the continuing care of previously existing polygamous wives and concubines.

In the same law another reform changed another time-honoured ancient Chinese custom. Marriages arranged by parents without consultation with the youngsters concerned had been the general rule throughout the ages in China. Chiang Kai-shek's government tried to change this by persuasive public propaganda, but failed. In the 1950 legislation the Communist leaders abolished the practice in large measure. One of its articles proclaimed that young men and women should be free to choose their own mates. In fact the reason for marriage began to be love between them, not some other consideration which served the interests of their elders. Naturally that very radical change did not spread swiftly throughout the conservative countrysides, where deeply rooted tradition could not vanish overnight; but it was widely welcomed by the young generation in urban areas, and had later extended in considerable measure almost everywhere. Both in 1962 and 1971 I discussed the question with several youthful wedded couples, and also with their parents. They all agreed that the reform was a blessing which greatly reduced quarrellings between the two different generations and also between members of the opposite sexes of the same generation in their family lives.

Opposite top : A creche in a Beijing commune gives mothers freedom to work

Opposite bottom : A young orchestra practises in the Children's Palace, Shanghai, where children can study creative subjects including painting. The example above shows the artistic freedom which the younger generation enjoy

The new law also permitted divorces when marriages turned out to be very unhappy. The first result of this was an immense spate of such separations by couples who had been victims of the old system of arranged marriages. Afterwards the numbers of divorces rapidly declined.

Mao's code of proper moral conduct also urged that husbands and wives should be faithful to one another, and disapproved of sexual relations existing between people outside marriage. One of the most astonishing facts about China in and around 1971 was that this principle was apparently wholly (or was it in fact only very nearly wholly?) accepted in practice throughout the land – an almost incredible difference from the China which I had known two decades earlier, as well as from the contemporary situation in various other lands. On one occasion when I ventured to ask a group of young early twenty-year-olds whether anyone in China engaged in "free love" they answered, "Oh no; that is a nasty capitalist custom".

In conformity with this ethical policy, very soon after the Communist government assumed office in 1949 prostitution was made illegal. Brothels everywhere were closed, and their scores of thousands of whores were taken to new institutions where they were cured of their venereal disease, rid of their inferiority complex, taught respectable new occupations, and then given good fresh jobs. Many of them got married, and we hope lived happily ever after. I trust that my young teenage "sing song girl" friend of 1929 was one of them.

These were some aspects of a Puritanical mood which had affected the Chinese people – including the entire young generation – since the Revolution. Others abounded. As a result of Mao's teaching the once widespread indulgence in opium-smoking had ceased; drug-taking, except when necessary for medical reasons, was unknown; gambling and pornography were unheard of; and a lot of thieving also seemed to have been stopped. Residents in hotels could certainly leave money, jewellery, gold watches and any other valuable possessions around in unlocked rooms with no risk of them disappearing. However, I am told that petty thefts did still continue among the Chinese themselves.

Another tremendous change in the Chinese way of life was the introduction of family planning. For various reasons which I need not analyse here most Chinese parents in earlier times had thought it advantageous to have numerous children. Often their babies multiplied almost like flies. Now birth control was encouraged, and married couples were advised (and indeed urged) to have no more than one or two children. The limitation was optional, not compulsory; but as a result of intensive official propaganda it was quite widely practised. Medical advice regarding it, plus efficient contraceptives, were available free in the health clinics in every factory and village – but only for giving to wedded pairs. The exceptional sections of the population among whom family planning was not encouraged were the small "minority nationalities", who were free to have as many infants as they wished.

A typical individual case of the practice was that of a 23-years-old waitress in a guest-house where I stayed in 1962. She had been married for three years to a captain in the army. When I asked her how many children they had, she laughed and replied, "Of course, none".

In answer to my next question "Why?" she said that her own education was not yet completed. She had been to a primary school, but no middle school; so now she attended a two-hour evening class three times each week after her day's work was done. By this means she had completed her junior middle school course of tuition, and was now starting on the senior course.

"How can I have children before I myself have finished schooling?" she asked.

And she added emphatically that she and her husband would not have more than two children, for they must not produce more than they could look after properly.

Again, these ideas had not penetrated far into the rural communes in 1962; but on my travels in 1971 I found that they were then more widely practised. Virtually all the young urban couples who had got married in the last dozen years were limiting their infants to one, two, or just occasionally three; and many of those in the rural areas were gradually moving towards a similar attitude. However, for economic reasons numerous peasant parents wished to have more children than three.

A reason why couples in the cities and towns occasionally wished to have more than two youngsters was illustrated during a chat which I had one day with a guide who was taking me on a tour of an industrial area. When I asked him whether he was married he replied, "Yes". When I then enquired whether he and his wife had any children he again answered in the affirmative.

"How many?" I asked.

"Three" he said.

Young people adjust complicated model aeroplanes and ships at the Children's Palace, Shanghai

I expressed surprise because of the customary family planning limit of two. But I added, "Does this mean that your two elder children were girls?".

"Yes" he answered with a smile.

"Did your wife succeed in making the third a boy?".

"Yes" he answered again with a merry laugh. "Now we'll have no more babies".

As part of the policy of family planning, since 1962 there had been a change in the customary ages of marriage. One of the reforms introduced in 1950 was the abolition of child betrothals. The new law laid down then that males could only marry after they were 20 years old and females after they were 18; and in 1962 I noticed that they often became brides and bridegrooms in their early twenties. Now, in 1971, official propaganda suggested that it was better for women to wait until they were about 25 and for men to wait until they were about 27 years old – a suggestion which had been widely adopted in the urban, but not in the rural areas.

As a result of all these moves the government's wish to ensure an enormous reduction in the rate of population growth was to some, but not a great, extent being realized. Another consequence of the changes in the last two decades was partly responsible for slowing that reduction. In an earlier chapter I mentioned that prior to 1949 the usual age of death for the overwhelming majority of the Chinese people was about 50 years. As a result of their better nourishment as well as of the new health services the infant mortality rate had now very greatly declined, and old people also stayed alive much longer. The figure of about 50 years had jumped to about 70 years.

I regretted some other features of contemporary China besides the too regimented reciting of Mao's Thoughts – however wise a lot of those thoughts might be. For example, I did not enjoy the noisy radio gossip and music which often filled the air in public parks and village fields, as well as in workshops, restaurants and railway carriages. The peace and quiet of Nature frequently got shattered by the blarings of broadcast programmes, no doubt many of them dispensing ideological propaganda in one way or another. Indeed, most of my criticisms sprang from what I regarded as too constant a preoccupation with such political indoctrination. This was not because it was Communist in its nature: I would have objected just as strongly if it were of any other radical, liberal or conservative dogma.

In that connection, I was sorry that the old classical Beijing operas and various similar provincial theatrical plays which had for centuries been dramatic expressions of Chinese culture had now got banished from the scene. I had watched them still being performed to large, delighted audiences in 1962; but about two years later their production was stopped. Instead, new operas portraying heroic episodes and characters in recent triumphant Communist events were enacted on stages behind the floodlights. The reason for this substitution was of course also political – to turn the theatre-going public's attention from romances of the nasty feudal past to deeds of the splendid Communist present. Some of the new productions were attractive as well as interesting; but it was a pity that the ancient and modern drama could not both live side by side. I hoped, and expected, that the older ones would be revived later, when the authorities did not feel it so essential to concentrate everyone's attention on the Marxist–Leninist–Maoist interpretation of human affairs.

A pavilion by Wuxi lake

A similar restoration could never occur in the case of certain other antique relics which had recently disappeared from sight. I remembered riding along Beijing's streets in 1929 on a frisky Mongolian pony, and approaching a massively handsome medieval gate-tower in the old Tartar city's fortress wall through which one of the caravans of camels bringing goods from the Gobi Desert was sauntering. Perhaps inevitably those camels no longer enlivened the scene; swifter-moving heavy motor vehicles had taken their places. But need the historic gateway also have vanished? It was true that some other splendid old gate-towers were still carefully preserved in surviving fragments of the wall elsewhere; but I wondered whether it was really necessary to knock down so much of the rest of the wall, including that grand fortification. Perhaps it was, and I was being too sentimental about bits and pieces of dead history. Certainly the broad, beautifully tree-lined highways for sophisticated twentieth century traffic which had taken their places since an important new era of history started in 1949 were impressive new assets in the capital.

Moreover, the contemporary Chinese government was doing a great deal to preserve other splendid ancient monuments, as I shall describe later.

8 A Shift in Foreign Policy

DURING MY STAY IN BEIJING IN 1971 I HAD A HAPPY TALK WITH MARSHAL CHEN YI IN A hospital where he had been confined for about a year as a patient suffering from cancer. Nominally still China's Foreign Minister, he was in fact too ill to do any work. Nevertheless throughout our conversation he was charmingly cheerful; and when I was about to leave he said that on my next visit to China he would be hale and hearty, and that he would guide me on a boat trip up the Yangtse River and through its famous gorges, which I had never yet seen.

On the following day I had a long talk with Zhou Enlai. In the course of it he confided to me that Chen Yi's cancer was probably incurable, and that, unknown to Chen Yi himself, he might soon be dead.

My delightful "twin" died early in the following year.

During Chen Yi's long period in hospital Zhou Enlai had been acting as China's Foreign Minister as well as its Premier. My talk with him continued for four hours, and covered not only certain aspects of the current situation inside the People's Republic of China, but also its government's attitude to current external affairs.

Most important among various developments which had occurred in its external relations since our discussions in 1962 was a shift in the Chinese leaders' attitude towards the United States of America. Their anxiety about a possible American aggression against their country had passed away. This was because of the complete failure of the Americans' fighting support for the South Vietnamese. As a consequence of that defeat President Nixon had recently declared his government's plan to withdraw all its armed forces from Vietnam, and also to reduce the American military presence elsewhere in the Far East.

Huang Hua, the Foreign Minister welcoming Malcolm MacDonald to Beijing in March 1979

As soon as it became evident that the President really meant what he said the Chinese attitude towards the United States began to relax. Indeed, Zhou Enlai told me that a few months later Chairman Mao and he were going to hold talks with the American President during a visit which Nixon proposed to pay to Beijing. Zhou emphasized that the Chinese had not invited him to come there, but that when a message from the White House in Washington hinted at the idea, and it got confirmed during Kissinger's recent visit to Beijing, they raised no objection. Zhou commented that they did not expect any substantial accord with the American government to result from the meeting because of the Americans' continuing diplomatic and military support for Chiang Kai-shek's regime in Taiwan. Nevertheless they thought that the contact could be a first step in a slow advance towards better relations between the two countries. Zhou added with a broad grin that he and his colleagues realized that one of Nixon's purposes in coming to Beijing was to gain prestige with sections of the voters prior to the next Presidential Election in the U.S.A., for he was eager still to be the President in the White House in 1976 when the 200th Anniversary of American Independence would be celebrated. Nixon would therefore no doubt be eager for a genially worded communiqué to be issued at the end of the visit. In those circumstances the Chinese might be able to get some partially useful concession in policy from him, without having to make any serious concession in return.

Zhou then told me that this development had potential significance in connection with another movement in international affairs which had occurred since our meetings in 1962. The Chinese government's fear of aggression by a foreign power had been switched from the possible enemy America to the probable enemy Russia. In fact the Americans had been demoted from the position of Enemy Number One to that of Enemy Number Three. The Russians were promoted to the top post, whilst the Japanese were regarded as Enemy Number Two. The latter status of Japan was due to the fact that the then militarist government in Tokyo not only still retained an Ambassador in Taiwan but also perhaps nursed an ambition at some future time to prevent Taiwan from being reunited with China by invading it and turning it into a Japanese dependency.

Zhou described to me how seriously relations between the two principal Communist nations had further deteriorated since they first started to become bad after the Russians' withdrawal of all their economic and technical aid to China. Through the last few years the Chinese had been trying to hold meaningful negotiations with the Russians to settle outstanding disputes concerning their very lengthy common frontier. But the Moscow authorities had obstinately resisted these attempts. This made the Chinese suspicious that the expansionist ambitions of the masters in the Kremlin made them so nervous about the steadily growing strength of their huge, potentially powerful Asian neighbour that they would launch a military attack against it whilst it was still comparatively weak. Zhou told me that this apprehension was reinforced by the fact that the Russians had stationed vast numbers of armed troops and a considerable amount of sophisticated military equipment along the frontier.

Chinese plannings for the nation's military defence were therefore now being devised more against the possibility of a Russian than of an American invasion. Fear of an assault by near-by Russia was, for example, the reason for the intensive building of air-raid shelters in all the regions of the country, which I told Zhou that I observed being done in various places during my recent widespread travels. I had learned that every factory, school, residential area and other populated spot in the cities and towns, and almost every village in the countryside now possessed such shelters. Only in mountainous areas where Nature provided effective cover were they not being built.

Zhou confirmed that this information was correct. He said that for the same reason the army, navy and air force were being kept in fighting trim, the militia everywhere underwent constant training, and the young Red Guards in colleges and schools did energetic semi-military physical exercises. The government believed that their whole people must be ready to offer strong resistance wherever the enemy might attack. I had seen evidence of this in a middle school that I visited, where I watched a company of boys and girls being taught how to hurl hand-grenades.

The authorities in Beijing naturally recognized Russia's immense military power, and its capacity to gain at least initial successes in a suddenly declared war. So they realized that the foe might well temporarily conquer whole Provinces. This was one reason why they were doing everything they could not only to settle large populations for resistance in their western and northern frontier regions, but also to make every Province, and even county, as far as possible economically self-reliant by the development within it of mining, light and heavy industries, increasing agricultural productivity, massive grain storage, and other needs.

Harking back a few years, Zhou complained about the conduct of the Russians in another matter. He said that Nehru's complacent refusal to enter into negotiations with him about the Indian–Chinese border problem before the outbreak of the short war in 1962 had been partly Kruschev's fault. At that time (according to information

received by the Chinese) the Soviet leader had urged on Nehru, "Don't make any concession to the Chinese about your frontier, and don't bother to talk with them about it. They won't fight, and so you've nothing to fear".

I felt sure that all the military preparations which the Chinese were making were still for national defence, not external offence. It was true that a sentence in a then recently published official statement of their government's foreign policy which reiterated that they favoured "peaceful co-existence between countries having different social systems" could be contradicted by a later sentence in it which asserted that they would "support and assist the revolutionary struggle of all the oppressed peoples and

Above : Ice-cream is popular throughout China even on the coldest days

Opposite : Children group behind their banner when visiting the Summer Palace

Visitors rest during a visit to the Imperial Palace

nations". However, the more precise significance of the latter broad statement had been spelt out in greater detail in other authoritative declarations. In a speech by an important member of the government, for example, he had said, "Of course, every revolution in a country stems from the demands of its own people. Only when the people in a country are awakened, mobilized, organized and armed can they overthrow the reactionary rule of imperialism and its lackeys through struggle; their role cannot be replaced or taken over by any people from any country outside . . . Revolution cannot be imported". He added "This does not exclude mutual sympathy and support on the part of revolutionary peoples in their struggles".

What did that "mutual sympathy and support" mean in practice? Mostly moral

A family picnic in the Summer Palace

support – the encouragement given to other revolutionaries by China's Communist victory, the lessons taught to them by Mao Zedong's published writings, and in some cases diplomatic, propagandist or economic help. The authorities in Beijing did not rule out completely the possibility of material support in the form of military aid; but, so far at least, this had continued to be almost entirely confined to the case of the Vietminh, for the mainly defensive reason that I have already described. Sometimes, when they were invited to lend such aid in a very limited way elsewhere – not involving their fighting troops – they were now ready to consider doing so, as I shall mention in one case later.

The sincerity of the Chinese attitude towards peaceful co-existence was illustrated

Above : The Imperial Vault of Heaven in the Temple of Heaven complex in Beijing

Opposite : A gateway in the Imperial City, Beijing

to me in a talk which I had with another old friend in Beijing in 1971. Prince Norodom Sihanouk of Cambodia had recently been banished from his kingdom by the "coup d'état" instigated by General Lon Nol with American encouragement. The Prince was now settled in the Chinese capital, where he had formed his government-in-exile.

He told me that when he was originally appointing his Ministers some of them suggested to him that it would be prudent to name their team "The People's Government of Cambodia". He felt averse to that idea, since the description could make many otherwise prospective supporters of the administration, both inside and outside Cambodia, suspect it of being a Communist-inclined government – a character which he had no intention that it should assume. The advocates of the suggestion continued to urge it, agreeing with him that their government should of course not be a Communist one, but expressing the opinion that the title would be a clear indication that its members intended to restore democratic civilian rule in Cambodia as opposed to the military autocracy established by Lon Nol. They also felt that the name would please the Chinese.

One day (Sihanouk continued to tell me) whilst the question was still unsettled Zhou Enlai came to see him. The Prime Minister said that he had heard that some of

123

the Prince's Ministers thought their team should be described as the People's Government of Cambodia. "Do you agree with that suggestion?" he asked.

"No", answered Sihanouk.

Zhou expressed strong support for his opposition. He stated that the Cambodians were not Communists: they were devoted Monarchists, devout Buddhists and conservatively non-Communist in political outlook. The suggested name for the government would therefore cause misunderstanding and arouse hostility against it among the Cambodian people. Zhou felt that for these reasons the Ministerial group-in-exile should assume the traditional title of "The Royal Government of Cambodia". He said that the Chinese authorities would not wish a Communist or any other form of government to be imposed on the Cambodians against their will. They believed that every national people in South East Asia should be free to choose whatever political type of government they themselves favoured, so that its authorities pursued policies which gained their approval and thus maintained contentment and peace in the land. He added that he and his colleagues in Beijing would only wish that in international affairs the Royal Government of Cambodia, and the other governments throughout the region, would be non-aligned between the two super-nations and their allies in the "cold war", seeking to maintain good relations with both groups.

Zhou commented to Sihanouk that the title "Royal Government" for his party of Ministers lodged in China would, incidentally, be helpful to the Chinese authorities. It would be a piece of evidence that they were genuine in their statements that every people round the world should be free to choose whatever form of government they wished, and in their advocacy of peaceful co-existence between nations practising different social systems.

I have already mentioned that another reason why the Chinese felt content to live in peaceful co-existence with all the other nations through the present period of time was that they believed that socialist revolutions were on the way throughout the world, brewing not only in other parts of Asia, Africa and South America but also in Europe, North America and everywhere else. Perhaps a score of years earlier they had reckoned that the process would be more rapid than it was turning out to be. If that was so, it was one of the miscalculations which they made, one of their mistakes from which they were learning. But whatever their earlier reckonings may have been, they were ready to be patient and pragmatic in their dealings with foreign affairs. For the Chinese, who had been civilized in one way or another through several millenia, a hundred years is rather like a hundred days. They were prepared to wait for other peoples to shift spontaneously into a rebellious mood. In the meantime they were determined to concentrate their own principal energies and resources on building up China's national strength.

Their national economy had by now advanced to a point at which their government could give financial and technical aid to some of the under-developed countries overseas. The principal example of this was in East Africa, where large sums of their money and considerable numbers of their technical engineers and skilled workers were being lent on extremely generous terms to Tanzania and Zambia to assist in the building of the lengthy TanZam railway. Nor was that their only activity in Tanzania. At the invitation of the government in Dar-es-Salaam they were aiding in the provision of military equipment and of training for the Tanzanian army. Moreover, in certain camps there some of their experienced soldiers were also helping to train Mozambiquan guerrilla

No railway journey is too short for cups of green China tea

fighters who would later join in the armed rebellion which had already broken out
against Portuguese colonial rule in next-door Mozambique.

In connection with the world-wide international situation Zhou expressed to me
his delight at the prospect of Britain joining the European Common Market. He
mentioned that he had been very pleased to hear in a recent BBC news broadcast that
our Prime Minister, Edward Heath, had made a speech at a Conservative Party
conference strongly favouring that plan. He hoped that the policy would soon be
carried out in practice, for a united Europe which included Britain could become an
international force of considerable strength. It could help distinctly to reduce the hitherto

overwhelmingly mighty influence of the two super-powers, America and Russia. Zhou remarked that the Chinese government would happily engage in good co-operative relations with such a Europe.

In connection with all this one of the Chinese leaders' earlier strong resentments against some of the Western Powers had been recently removed. The authorities in Beijing had continued to feel deeply offended by the exclusion of the People's Republic of China from the United Nations Organization, and by the inclusion of Taiwan among its members instead, as if the Kuomintang regime there was the legitimate government of China. They nursed their indignation mostly in private, pretending that they did not regard the U.N. as a very important body – an attitude which was no doubt prompted by the old trait in the Chinese character of wishing to "save face".

Shortly before my visit to Beijing in 1971, however, the People's Republic had at last been admitted into the United Nations. This was one of the signs of the increasing recognition by many other governments round the world of Communist China's growing importance in contemporary human affairs.

Through the next few months that recognition became steadily more evident. Early in 1972 President Nixon's proposed visit to Beijing took place. As Zhou had anticipated, it did not result in any very substantial improvement in relations between their two countries because the American government continued to maintain diplomatic relations with, as well as to give military and economic aid to, Chiang Kai-shek's regime in Taiwan. But at the same time the Chinese agreed to accept an American "liaison officer" in Beijing and to appoint a Chinese "liaison officer" to Washington – which was a real step forward. A better mutual understanding between their two nations began to develop.

A significant little, and potentially big, piece of new history had been made.

9 Ancient Monuments

MY NEXT VISIT TO CHINA OCCURRED IN JUNE 1975. I LED A DELEGATION OF BRITISH ART gallery and museum experts who went to view a lot of the archaeological and artistic treasures recently excavated there, and to discuss important matters of common concern with their erudite Chinese fellow scholars on the subject.

During my travels through the country four years earlier I had seen several examples of the fine work that the government in Beijing was doing not only to preserve but also to restore to their original architectural grandeur splendid historical monuments, such as part of the Great Wall of China, some of the Ming Tombs and the Imperial Palace in the Forbidden City in Beijing. These had all fallen into considerable disrepair during the periods of the Warlords' and the Kuomintang's rules.

A typical example was the serenely beautiful Temple of Heaven on the outskirts of Beijing. When I had first set eyes on it in 1929 it was lovely, but in a somewhat sad state of dilapidation. It continued to be so in 1948. When I visited it again in 1962 an impressive amount of repair was already being done, and in 1971 a superb work of restoration had been completed on its very gracious central shrine. I gazed with admiration at the sacred temple. In feudal times the reigning Emperor had come there on a special occasion each year to pray for a continuation of the blessings of Heaven on his Imperial Realm. It had now been painstakingly and skilfully repaired so that it looked exactly the same as it had done in those feudalistic days when he went there to worship. Every detail of its original gorgeously carved and colourfully painted and gilded decorations had been renewed with majestic splendour – including the five claws on the feet of its dragons which showed that they were Imperial stooges!

Similar restorations were being made in other ancient monuments throughout China. Unfortunately many lovely old temples, pagodas and other such buildings had been allowed to fall into a state of disrepair from which they could not be rescued.

It was also true that during the Cultural Revolution wild gangs of political extremists had damaged some other attractive relics of old culture, condemning them as remnants of feudalism. But many of the noblest antiquities and finest collections of classical artistic works were protected then by militia units, on the orders of the authorities. They were regarded as precious creations by the exploited workers of bygone ages which their present-day liberated descendants should treat with great respect.

One result of the industrial and agricultural development which had been taking place all across the land was a great impetus given to excavations by archaeologists and other researchers into early Chinese history and civilization. At diggings made for the construction of new roads, irrigation canals, industrial towns, airfields and other modern enterprises large numbers of buried antique relics had been unearthed. As soon as any such object was revealed by a plunge of a spade or other implement into the ground the work was stopped, nearby appropriate academic authorities were at once informed, and they then came and directed the resumed diggings in proper scientific ways from the point of view of extracting unharmed the ancient treasure. In addition all the peasants in the communes were told that whenever they happened to catch sight of old bits of pottery, bronzes or other such finds as they toiled in the fields they must extract them very carefully and hand them over intact to the authorities. They did this faithfully.

Many of the learned archaeologists and related scholarly men and women told me during my visits in 1962 and 1971 that they were receiving more assistance from the present government than they or their predecessors had ever done within living memory. As a result of all these activities scores of thousands of hitherto buried remains were added to the nation's collections. All the finds were treated expertly. And many public art galleries and museums – including large numbers of new ones established during the last twenty years – were exhibiting hoards of recently discovered treasures. Among them were numerous bits of fossilized skulls of contemporaries of Beijing Man who had lived about 500,000 years ago, hand-tools and other utensils from the sites of variously aged prehistoric settlements, and many, many thousands of works of art and handicrafts belonging to every Dynastic epoch that had occurred during the last four millennia. These included, for instance, the regal costumes and other decorative palatial ornaments found in the Ming Emperor Wan Li's recently opened tomb. Other typical discoveries were antique silks, iron weights, instruments for astronomy and calendar-making, and books on all sorts of subjects such as agriculture, medicines and the sciences. Among them was the earliest manuscript copy of *The Analects of Confucius* so far found, dated A.D. 710.

In 1971 I visited an exhibition of many of the ancient works of art which had been unearthed during the last several years, and which were on display for the public in the Winter Palace in Beijing. They were housed in the rooms of pavilions that used to be the residences of retired ex-concubines of the current Emperor, ladies who had grown too old to perform their principal duty for him. How appropriate it was that the place should once more be a home for antique beauties, although its latest occupants

A pagoda in the Summer Palace which was first built in 1153 by the Emperor Wan Yan Liang and was restored, after a long history of destruction and rebuilding by the Dowager Empress in 1888. Preservation is high on the priority of the authorities today

Above : The figure of Guanyin, Goddess of Mercy, behind the Great Buddha in the Zhao Qing Si Temple, Hangzhou
Opposite : The Temple of the Jade Buddha, Shanghai

were fashioned in bronze, silver, gold, porcelain or other materials instead of in human flesh!

Among them were some unique pieces. Perhaps the most remarkable of these were the now famous pair of costumes made of jade in the shapes of life-size human beings, which had covered the corpses of a Western Han prince and his princess when they were buried more than 2,000 years ago. Constructed to serve the same purpose as the mummy-cases of dead Pharaohs in early Egypt, one of them was composed of 2,690 and the other of 2,156 small oblong bits of exquisitely carved jade, all sewn together with gold thread.

Overleaf: The Temple of the Azure Clouds outside Beijing. It contains 508 lifelike statues of Lohans, Buddhist saints

The famous marble boat built by the Dowager Empress Ci Xi with funds intended for China's antiquated navy

It is perhaps needless to add that many of those "objets d'art" were used partly for Communist propaganda purposes. A descriptive note attached alongside each one of them in the display cabinets stated not only its age, purpose and artistic merit but sometimes also the social circumstances in which it was made. Many of the exhibits were thus presented as evidence of the brilliant craftsmanship of the poor workers who created them for the selfish enjoyment of the rich rulers in the tyrannical past. For instance, after an excellent informative account of the historic importance of the jade human figures mentioned above the description of them added that they were "a penetrating exposure of the idle and extravagant life of the feudal ruling class based on their cruel oppression and exploitation of the labouring people".

During our travels in 1975 my art museums companions and I were able to study very closely many, many such recently rediscovered relics of the ancient past, and to discuss their significance with the top Chinese authorities on the subject. Among the places which we visited were the cave where Beijing Man dwelt 500,000 years ago, a similar abode in which Upper Cave Man resided about 18,000 years ago, the recently excavated more than 6,000 years old Neolithic village of Banpo near Xian, some of the Longmen (Lung-men) caves containing sculptures of various periods in the feudal era, newly unearthed Tang (T'ang) tombs at Qianlong (Ch'ien-ling) such as the burial vault of the renowned Empress Wu, ancient and now well restored gardens of the Song (Sung), Yuan, Ming and Qing dynastic periods in Suzhou (Soochow), and museums filled with a great variety of fascinating and often beautiful objects in Beijing, Nanjing, Shanghai, Guangzhou and several other places. Most of their exhibits had been unearthed during the last twenty-five years. We learned that the most antique very recent find was a pair of fossilized teeth from some primeval human being who had lived sometime between one and three million years ago. The experts had not yet been able to make sufficient tests to establish their more or less precise antiquity. This was later revealed to be about 1,700,000 years.

In some of the mountainous country in the north we saw sights which seemed to bring the ancient past partly back to life. Many peasant families still lived in caves, some of which had been continuously inhabited since at least Ming and even Song times. Those homes were cut into the high cliff-like sides of lofty hills. In their cavernous rooms a few chairs, tables, beds and household goods stood around, no doubt giving the residents more comfort than Beijing Man and his descendants had enjoyed. And if a visitor nevertheless felt that he must have slipped back thousands of years into the past, a sudden blare of radio talk from a box hanging on a rocky wall assured him that he was still alive in the twentieth century A.D.

During our journeys I saw that a great deal of more extended and beautifully accomplished restoration work had been done along a part of the Great Wall, in the Forbidden City, at the Temple of Heaven, through the Summer Palace and at many other historic sites since I last gazed enchanted at them in 1971.

Everywhere that we went my erudite British colleagues discussed with similarly learned Chinese savants the latest methods of conserving fragile relics of bygone ages such as old scroll-paintings, and they exchanged their professional experiences and the most up-to-date information on various specialist matters. In the course of those scholarly talks we were shown many particularly important treasures which had been taken out of storage especially for us to see, including newly unearthed bronzes, ceramics, lacquer-wares and other "objets d'art" which had not yet been viewed by anyone except the Chinese authorities concerned. It was exciting not only to see them with our eyes but also to be able to touch them with our hands.

Whilst we were in Xian we heard an enthralling piece of news. One day in the previous year a group of farm workers digging a well had suddenly, by chance, exposed part of a pit which might contain some very antique art treasures because the site was in the valley of the Yellow River about a mile from the 150 feet high man-made hill called Mount Li which late in the Third Century B.C. was constructed above the tomb of the famous Emperor Chin Shih-huang-ti, who had then by military conquests transformed the several Warring States into the first widespread united China. The task of excavating the pit had therefore been handed over to archaeologists.

Opposite : The Hall of Prayer for Good Harvests in the Temple of Heaven complex, where the Emperor prayed each spring

Above : The Hung Qian Dian, the Temple of the August Heavens where the tablets of dead Emperors were kept

Below : One of the bronze lions in the Imperial Palace

The news that we received was that they had very recently begun to unearth an array of statuesque life-size terracotta figures of soldiers and horses which were about 2,200 years old – a very exciting discovery.

To bring that story up-to-date, through the next five years the excavations continued, and they will proceed for many years to come, for only a few recesses of the total underground site have so far been explored. It is now reckoned that the whole area covers more than three acres of ground, and that it was filled with about 6,000 terracotta soldiers and more than 400 terracotta horses drawing over 100 wooden chariots – a formidable army marshalled to guard the Emperor lying in his near-by tomb against

A painted pottery tomb model of acrobats, dancers and musicians, entertaining courtiers and officials found in 1969. Western Han Dynasty

138

possible enemies. The wooden chariots have all disintegrated, and many of the statues were broken into fragments by marauding grave robbers in ancient times. But many of them still survive intact, except that the paint which originally made them look rather like living men and steeds has faded away. Yet they remain vivid, each human figure being somewhat different from every other, with slightly differing postures or facial expressions. In addition many metal swords, spear-heads and bits of other weapons, and also gold, bronze, jade or other kinds of utensils which were buried with them for their use still lie around uncorroded, as do the metal fittings of the horses' bridles and the chariots' wheels.

Bronze horses from the tomb at Leitai, reminders of the power of the Han cavalry which campaigned during that dynasty

Below : The famous jade suit that once covered the body of Prince Liu Sheng, one of the thirteen sons of the Emperor Qing who died in 141 BC

Opposite : Gilt bronze statue of a servant girl holding a lamp, found in the tomb of Princess Dou Wan, consort of Prince Liu Sheng

To anticipate for a moment, when I visited the National Historical Museum in Beijing in 1979 I saw some of those very handsome warriors and horses assembled on parade in a gallery there – wonderful survivors of the brilliantly creative artistic civilization which thrived in China more than four thousand years ago.

To jump back to 1975, my travelling companions and I were taken on visits not only to ancient monuments and museums filled with antique treasures, but also to modern institutes where living artists and handicraftsmen were brushing scroll-paintings, carving jade and ivory, sewing needlework adornments, designing shell-decoration pictures, and creating other aesthetic works. They showed superb skills, which had of course been handed down to them from generation to generation through centuries. Occasionally however (and I sometimes thought regrettably) in such operations as jade carving they used small modern mechanized implements instead of hand-tools. In other cases modern innovations brought improvements to their artistic creations. For instance, "since Liberation" (I kept being told) the differing colours and shades of cotton and silk threads used by the needle-workers in the decorative embroidery institutions had been greatly increased in number and variety, with many beautiful results. This was one of numerous signs of the stimulating encouragement being given by the government to the arts in contemporary China. Many of the artists' products were designed in traditional styles portraying Imperial dragons, phoenixes and other such creatures, whilst many others illustrated in modern fashion the Revolutionary achievements of the Red soldiers, workers and peasants in the new Chinese People's Republic.

10 Modern Progress Continues

OUR ALMOST NON-STOP SUCCESSION OF ENGAGEMENTS EVERY DAY THROUGH TWO WEEKS in 1975 were largely concentrated on viewing as many as possible of the archaeological and related artistic discoveries unearthed in China during the last quarter of a century. Nevertheless, as we journeyed by car, train or aeroplane from one place to another we caught many glimpses of various aspects of the young New China being created. I shall mention here a few representative examples of them.

One was the considerable amount of destruction of old slum-like hovels and the erection of neat new residences which had taken place in urban centres since my last visit four years ago. Many of the modern buildings rose high towards the sky, rather as the ancient pagodas did; but these novel constructions were not dwelling places for the gods. They were high-rise habitations filled with flats where the working people's families lived.

This was one sign of the increasing numbers of those workers in industries. Another was the much greater crowds of bicycles being pedalled along the streets in all the towns and cities. In Beijing, for example, I was told that the human population was now about 4,000,000 and the bicycle population about 2,000,000. Broad streams of bikes flowed along the highways carrying their riders to and from work. Nonetheless, numerous workers – presumably generally those paid the lowest grades of wages – still travelled to and from their factories squatting crowded on the floors of lorries, whilst others journeyed by bus. There were many more motor vehicles of various kinds in the city and its neighbourhoods than previously. Very rarely in the capital or its suburbs did one now see an animal-drawn, and still less a human-drawn, cart. In almost all the other urban centres, however, those vehicles continued to be tugged along the streets quite frequently.

The department stores in the cities and towns were filled with a greater variety, and

Above : Glazes being applied to china before firing in the Beijing Institute of Arts and Crafts

Below : Colourful hangings on sale in No. One Department Store, Shanghai

in some cases an improved quality, of consumer goods than had been available in 1971. Among them were more charming sorts of clothing: gaily coloured trousers, jerseys and stockings for children, blouses and dresses – but still not cheongsams – for girls and women, and shirts for men. Indeed, even the hues of the workers' and peasants' uniforms as they performed their daily jobs were no longer almost all dark grey or blue. Many of the teams of farm labourers toiling in the communes' fields, for instance, were a brighter sight than on my previous visits. Thus rows of women planting seeds wore a gay assortment of dark blue, light blue, green, red and light yellow jackets or blouses above their grey trousers.

More mechanical implements, tractors and other machines were helping the peasants in their work in the fields. At the same time throughout the rural countrysides numerous carts drawn sometimes by horses, donkeys, mules or bullocks and at other times hauled by men or women still wandered slowly along the roads. But there were more motor vehicles and more pedal-bicycles than hitherto. Quite a larger number of peasants now owned the latter means of conveyance. Indeed, one member of a commune's Revolutionary Committee with whom I spoke told me that his family of five individuals possessed three bicycles. But usually a family owned only one, as I observed when a bicycle sometimes sped past me with a man sitting on its saddle, his wife seated on the carrier behind him, and their two children riding astride the rail in front of him. Occasionally I saw a third child in addition travelling as a passenger – a baby strapped to its mother's back as she sat on the carrier.

Just now and then a surprising new sight appeared – a motor-bicycle racing along a country road. I was told that this novel, and still very rare, phenomenon was not used by cadres or suchlike personages, for those bikes were too expensive for private ownership. They were ridden by postmen or other public servants going on official errands in widely scattered rustic areas.

An overwhelming majority of all the different kinds of vehicles, light and heavy machinery and other materials being used were now made in China, as were almost all the many varieties of goods for sale in the shops. The prices of those goods were still strictly controlled and mostly stabilized; but some of them – such as medicines and transistor radios – had been reduced again in the last few years.

All these facts were signs of a further slight improvement in the way of life of the masses of the people. Well informed members of the Diplomatic Corps in Beijing told me that the material standard of living of most of the people had risen slowly but definitely in the last few years. This was especially true of the poorest industrial workers, for the wages of the three lowest grades had been increased in 1972 – as had been hopefully anticipated by some authorities with whom I talked in 1971. The pay of the peasants in most, though not all, of the communes had also been somewhat increased. This was because of higher yields of crops in many regions, which meant that in those cases the communes' financial profits had considerably swollen. So a larger amount of the money could be allocated to wages for the farm labourers.

There were several reasons for this rise in profits. One was that progressively more efficient modern agricultural machinery was being used in the fields; another that better chemical fertilizers had been produced for distribution over the land; and another that in some regions two crops were being grown instead of one each year, whilst in other, usually tropical, regions three crops instead of two were being grown. Yet another reason was that, as a result of production in experimental State farms, several

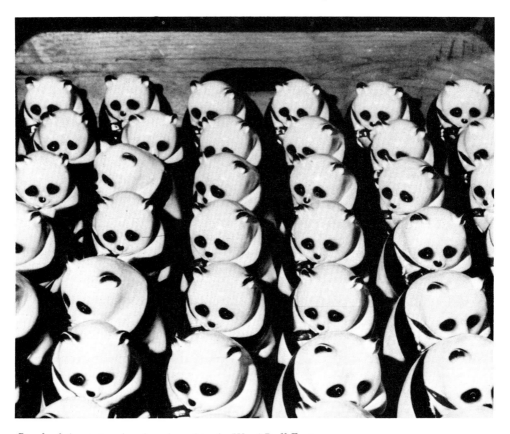

Pandas being painted and packaged in the Wuxi Doll Factory

better kinds of vegetables, fruits and other foodstuffs were being cultivated and more robust types of ducks, pigs and other animals were being bred in many communes. In addition numerous communes were making and repairing their own agricultural implements and other requirements in forges, foundries and small factories built in the rural towns and villages.

Moreover, although virtually no rain had fallen from the skies in very wide regions of the country during the last eight months, the great extension of reservoirs, irrigation canals and pumping stations on the ground had enabled the peasants to defy that drought and to gather vast harvests of grain and other produce.

I must mention another interesting fact. As the reader knows, one of the material incentives for hard labour by the peasants in the communes which had been reintroduced after a period of withdrawal was the ownership by individual families of small private plots of land. The authorities had nevertheless continued to urge that this should be a temporary expedient, and that when the villagers had been educated to become sincere believers in Mao's fully socialist Thoughts all such private ownership should be abolished. The whole land and all its produce should be the public property of the nation.

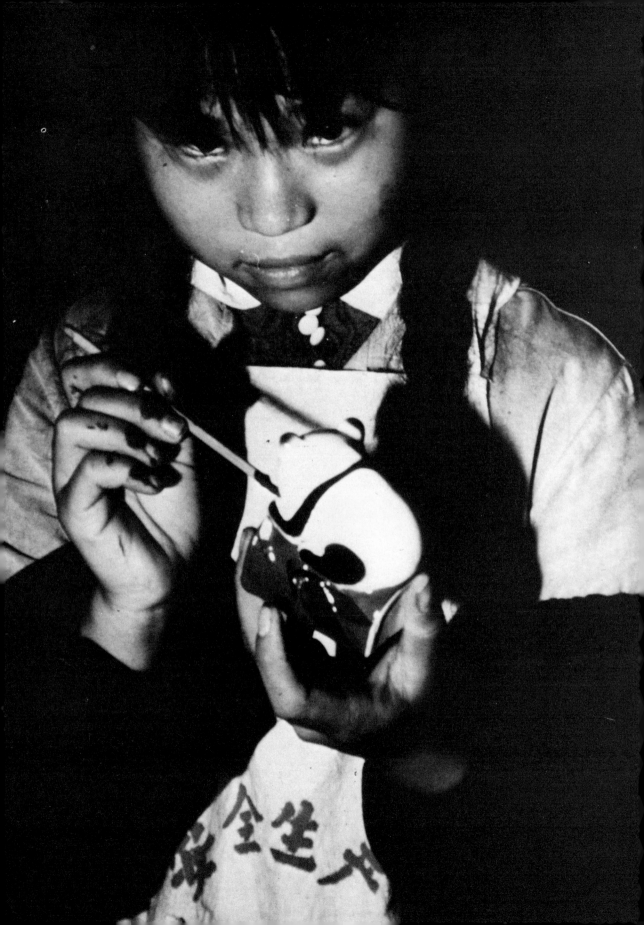

Statuettes of heroic dancers being made at the Wuxi Doll Factory

During my travels in China in 1971 I had learned that a rather remarkable event had recently occurred. The peasants in the famous commune at Dazhai had unanimously decided that the time had arrived when they should set an example by surrendering all their private plots and handing them back to collective ownership. Those rustics were proud to be members of a commune which was celebrated as a model farming community, and they no doubt took the new step partly to maintain that noble reputation. They wished to be the pioneers of this new desirable reform.

The event of course received a lot of favourable publicity; and the members of the Revolutionary Committees in several other communes wished to try to catch up with renowned Dazhai. Shortly afterwards some of them therefore also abolished the ownership of private plots in their collective farms – but those additional pioneers were very, very few in number! During my visit in 1975 I asked whether any more had followed suit – and the answer was in the negative. Progress towards a completely Communist society continued to be slow, in some ways hesitant, and even rather halting.

Occasionally I sensed a significant change of another kind hovering in the air. In talks with some intellectual enthusiasts about cultural matters they now and then expressed opinions which were not wholly consistent with the usually dogmatic

Pandas being embroidered in the Children's Palace, Shanghai

Communist party viewpoints. They were evidently engaging in a little freedom of thought, and even of private speech. None of their remarks criticized the government's political, economic or social policies, but they sometimes described them in different, more relaxed language than the official jargon which on previous visits I had heard recited over and over again in precisely the same wording by everyone. And on other subjects their comments quite often hinted at slightly unorthodox individual ideas beginning to be bandied around.

A piece of evidence of this occurred during a conversation which my travelling companions and I had one day with an art gallery official. In his spare time he was an amateur artist, drawing and painting sketches. He told us that groups of artists quite often met together to talk about their work, and to discuss art problems in general. The groups were sometimes large gatherings of a hundred or more individuals, and at other times small companies of a dozen or less. In reply to a question as to whether those present at them ever disagreed with one another and held arguments about art styles, he replied enthusiastically "Yes". He said that everyone of those gatherings was free to express his or her opinions, and that often very vigorous controversies arose. And he remarked that it was time that the government returned to its earlier announced, short-lived and suddenly abandoned policy of – to quote Mao Zedong's words – "letting a hundred flowers blossom and a hundred schools of thought contend".

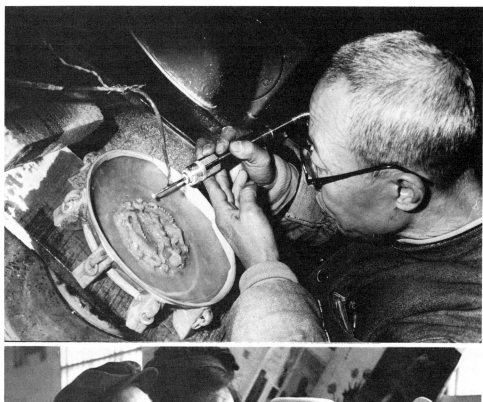

Old crafts, such as jade carving, top, are carried on using modern methods and master craftsmen in ceramics, below, pass on their knowledge to the younger generation

Zhou Enlai was sadly ill in a hospital then, and I could not see him.

I had a talk in Beijing with the Foreign Minister, Qiao Guanhua (Chiao Kuan-hua), who had succeeded Chen Yi in that office. He and I were old friends, for we had met several times in earlier years in various countries, and especially during the Conference on Laos in Geneva during the early 1960s. He was then Chen Yi's principal adviser in the Chinese delegation.

Now, in 1975, we discussed many aspects of the current international situation. Several changes had taken place in recent years in the South East Asian scene. Relations between China and some of the countries there had distinctly improved. About twelve months ago Malaysia had established diplomatic relations with the government in Beijing; a few months later the Philippines had followed suit; and Thailand was now on the point of doing the same. And although Indonesia and Singapore still refrained from adopting that policy, their governments were definitely non-aligned in the still simmering "cold war". Indeed, a while earlier the governments of those five independent countries had joined together in forming the Association of South East Asian Nations (ASEAN), which sought to develop regional economic and other co-operation between them in peaceful, progressive conditions which made it desirable for them to have friendly relations with all the potentially helpful external powers.

Qiao expressed pleasure at the better relations growing between China and Malaysia, the Philippines and Thailand; and he criticized the stand-offish attitude of Indonesia and Singapore. I told him (what I knew from talks with the Ministers responsible in those two lands) that this arose from their governments' continuing suspicion of the character and purpose of the Chinese authorities' support for rebel Communist movements in South East Asia; and I urged on him that the Beijing leaders should cease some of their present actions which aroused a belief that they were privately giving the insurgents material aid. Qiao defended those actions as ideologically natural, and stated emphatically that they consisted of purely moral, not material support.

In the other three countries in South East Asia changes were on the way which might lead in either a similar or a contrary direction. The situation in Vietnam was definitely contrary. The Vietminh forces had completed their conquest of the whole country, and its government was not simply ideologically sympathetic with the external Communist powers but also firmly aligned with Russia against America in international affairs.

In Cambodia General Lon Nol's pro-American regime still lingered in office in Phnom Penh, but political and military opposition forces were gaining such increasingly widespread successes that its days were numbered. However, although those forces were united in their aim of overthrowing Lon Nol's team, they held divided views about the nature of the government which should succeed it. The Khmer Rouge guerrilla fighters wanted the successor to be a Communist administration aligned against America, whereas Prince Sihanouk's government-in-exile wished it to be non-Communist in internal affairs and non-aligned in its external policy.

In Laos the coalition government (including a minority of Communist Ministers) which had ruled for many years following the Geneva Conference, and which was entirely non-aligned in its foreign policy, had fairly recently been replaced by a wholly Communist administration. Nevertheless that new government also had so far maintained friendly relations with the Western nations on one side and with China and Russia on the other.

151

Qiao agreed with me that it was to be hoped that the existing government in Laos and the future government in Cambodia would both become as firmly non-aligned in their external relations as were the five ASEAN countries. However, that prospect seemed uncertain because the Vietnamese Communist authorities sought to interfere in the internal affairs of those two weaker next-door states in ways which would not only make their leaders conform with Vietnam's international policy, but also indeed serve the Vietnamese rulers' ambition to become in effect the governors over those two other old Indo-Chinese countries.

Regarding wider world affairs Qiao expressed great pleasure that the British people had decided in a recent referendum that their nation should remain a member of the European Community. He was also glad that Britain at the same time maintained its membership of the widespread Commonwealth. He felt worried about the declining influence of the United States of America in efforts to settle international problems sensibly, and was alarmed at the consequent gradually growing influence of Russia in keeping those problems unsettled. He feared that large sections of American public opinion were now in a mood of disillusionment with peoples outside their own shores, and that they wished their nation to withdraw once more into a policy of isolationism in world affairs. This could be disastrous. He reckoned that the Americans' attitude resulted partly from a sense of disappointed frustration at the rather negative, unhelpful responses of some nations on the European continent to Washington's ideas, and he hoped that the British government would persuade those nations' governments to be more constructively co-operative with the Americans on matters about which the latter felt particular concern.

He kept reiterating his and his colleagues' conviction that the Russians planned by every possible means – secret, cunning and unscrupulous – to extend their influence steadily and ever more powerfully through the world, on one continent after another. He felt that the European peoples, including some of us British, did not appreciate this, nor recognize the growing military strength of Russia and the dangers which this threatened for them as well as for others. This was another fact of which he hoped that we British would become ourselves fully aware, and which we would persuade our European allies to recognize. We must all take the necessary counter actions.

In the context of Russia's ambitious plottings he spoke very critically of the Indian government's present policy of establishing close friendly relations with the Soviet rulers. He said that the Ministers in Delhi did not seem to realize that a main purpose of the masters in Moscow in fostering such a relationship was to use India as a corridor land through which they could establish more contacts with the peoples of Burma, Laos, Vietnam and beyond. This line of communication would help the Russians not only to make the South East Asian nations increasingly hostile to America, Europe and their associated states, but also to draw them on to the side of Russia against China in the quarrel which existed between those two Communist powers. It was all part of Moscow's strategy to establish eventual Russian domination all round the Earth.

When I expressed, sincerely, my complete agreement with his analysis of the Russians' intentions Qiao rose from his chair, came with both hands outstretched very friendlily towards me, and slapped me enthusiastically on the back.

11 Mao and Zhou Pass Away

AS I HAVE ALREADY MENTIONED, DURING MY STAY IN CHINA IN MID-1975 ZHOU ENLAI was very ill in hospital. He never recovered from the cancer that afflicted him, and in January 1976 he died. In September of the same year Mao Zedong also passed away. So the two supreme creators of the new China vanished almost simultaneously from the scene.

Their superb partnership had continued through more than fifty years, from the moment when in 1921 they were two of the early members of the Chinese Communist Party. Together they had made an extremely important piece of modern history. An oft-quoted aphorism states that "The hour produces the man." But in the case of the problem facing the vast, very antiquated Chinese nation in the early twentieth century one man, however Titanic a genius he might be, would not have been enough to conceive and carry into practice a right solution. A team of supremely able men was required to perform that formidable task; and fortunately the hour produced not simply the necessary man but the necessary men. Mao was the superlative radical political philosopher and strategist who by his preaching and leadership was more responsible than any other individual for promoting the Revolution; but without Zhou's pre-eminent gifts as a governmental administrator translating their policies into practice the colossal venture could have crashed in ruins. And even that pair of geniuses could not by themselves have achieved their gigantic aim; they needed other vital help from highly qualified colleagues in certain different fields of activity, such as General Zhu De, the fine military commander of their guerrilla warriors throughout the early, embattled years.

Mao's political creed which gave birth to The People's Republic of China was of course based on the Communist philosophy of Marx, Engels and to some extent Lenin; but without his important major adaptations of it to suit Chinese conditions it could

not have succeeded in that country. As I mentioned earlier, an essential element in Marx's teaching was that the class war must be waged by the industrial workers in the urban areas against their capitalist exploiters, but – contrary to the urgings of some of his Chinese comrades as well as of the Russians – Mao sought to gain victory by mobilizing instead the agricultural peasants in the rural areas against their landlord oppressors. It was as a result of that unorthodox strategy that not only the peasants but also in due course the workers secured proletarian power.

I have already recounted how remarkably the standard of living of the hundreds of millions of ordinary citizens in the villages, towns and cities alike had been raised by the time that I went to China in 1962 compared with what I had seen there as recently as 1948. It did not consist simply of more food and better household comforts which they enjoyed in their homes, but also of the new transport arrangements for them going to and from their work, the public health services available to them all, the education given to their children in schools, the recreation parks, sports grounds and cinema theatres available for their pleasure, and other to them wholly novel beneficial conditions. Their way of life was still in many respects extremely simple, but even so it was far pleasanter than any of them had ever imagined possible in their wildest dreams only a dozen years ago. The members of the old and middle-aged generations who remembered the miserable poverty which afflicted them before 1949 thought that a miracle had happened. And they recognized that the man who had performed the miracle was Chairman Mao. They therefore not only felt enormous gratitude to him but admired him to the point of virtual worship. It was for this reason that during and after the Cultural Revolution, when they were tutored in "The Thoughts of Chairman Mao" published in the *Little Red Book*, they and their growing-up youngsters wholly accepted every word that he wrote as the Truth, the whole Truth and nothing but the Truth. So the gospel according to Mao in both public and private affairs was, for some years, just about universally obeyed.

Looking forward then, one wondered whether the next young, rising generation of Chinese, who did not recall from their personal experience how miserably different life had been for almost all their fellow countrymen before the Revolution, would feel anything like the same faith in his teachings. No doubt changes loomed in the future.

I never had the privilege of meeting Mao Zedong. Zhou Enlai had planned for me to do so at the National Day Celebrations to be held in Beijing on October 1st, 1971; but a short while earlier the crisis springing from Lin Biao's attempted "coup d'état" erupted, and those celebrations were cancelled. Mao stayed away from the capital.

My friendship with Zhou Enlai was one of the greatest pleasures of my life. During my nearly four-score years on this Earth I have had the privilege of knowing quite a number of the truly great men working creatively in various fields of human activity in many different lands scattered across all the continents and seas. I think that Zhou was as fine a political statesman as any among them – which is saying a lot, for the others included such (for very varied reasons) immortal figures as Mahatma Gandhi in India, Franklin Roosevelt in America, Jomo Kenyatta in Kenya and Winston Churchill in Britain.

Opposite : Wreaths and poems by the workers of the Shukuang Electrical Machinery Plant in memory of Zhou Enlai

Zhou's greatness was not due simply to his superlative public qualities as a governor in national affairs and a diplomat in international affairs, performing the colossal task of guiding the re-emergence of China as a super-nation. It sprang also from his private personal character. He was a delightfully charming, highly intelligent and sincerely friendly man, endowed with self-confidence but at the same time unassuming modesty. None of his actions were inspired by selfish ambition. In spite of his outstanding abilities as a ruler he never entertained any wish to assume the top office in the state, as some of his colleagues conspired to do. Wholly loyal to Mao Zedong as their leader

A painting depicting Mao Zedong saying to Hua Guofeng 'With you in charge, I am at ease'

(in spite of occasional disagreements with him on matters of policy, when he fortunately usually managed sooner or later to persuade Mao to modify his attitude), he was happy to remain a lieutenant under the inspiring captain. He was completely, unselfishly dedicated to the service of the Chinese people.

My last meeting with him was the one that occurred during my stay in Beijing in 1971. Already then 73 years old, he was still robustly healthy in body, mind and spirit in spite of the ceaselessly onerous and often extremely difficult tasks which he had been performing non-stop as Prime Minister, and sometimes also Foreign Minister, through more than two decades. Late one night, when he had finished his customary day's toil, we met and talked from 10.30 o'clock in the evening until 3.15 a.m. in the small hours of the following morning.

Our discussion covered many contemporary Chinese and world-wide affairs. Concerned that he should go to bed for a rest before his next day's arduous work started, I every now and then said that I must leave him so that he could have a good sleep. But he always replied that our talk was so valuable that he would like it to continue.

Orderly queues wait to visit the immense mausoleum of Chairman Mao in Beijing

In fact he almost always retired to bed for only three or four hours each night. Incidentally in that connection I remember that when I was an undergraduate studying history at Oxford the erudite Professor L. B. Namier taught me something about Napoleon Buonaparte. At one point in a tutorial he asked me, "Do you know why Napoleon was such a very successful great man?"

I offered several suggestions, all of which Namier rejected.

When I asked him what was the real reason he answered that it was because the Emperor needed to sleep for only three or four hours each night – a brief interval of rest which enabled him to do several more hours of work every day than his contemporaries could do whilst they were absent in the Land of Dreams. So Napoleon was always ahead of them in his plannings and actions.

To skip back from Paris to Beijing, eventually in the early hours of the morning Zhou said reluctantly that we should go to bed, and I reluctantly agreed with him.

"When are you coming back to China?" he asked. "Come as often as you can. No one is more welcome here than you are".

I answered that I planned to return periodically every few years; and I added merrily that the visit to which I most looked forward was the one that I would pay in 1996. China's lease of Kowloon territory to Britain would then be within a year of running out, and I would greatly like to discuss with him the future of the British Colony of Hong Kong. "I expect you'll still be China's Prime Minister in 1996", I commented.

He laughed and replied, "No". Then he added, "I can't guarantee to be Prime Minister for more than another five years".

He made the statement emphatically, with an indication of his determination to remain in his eminent post for that further period of time. I gained an impression that he said it partly for the information of some high civil servants in the government who had been listening to our long conversation.

If that was his reason, the explanation could be that the quartet of politically extremist people headed by Mao Zedong's wife Jiang Qing (Chiang Ching), who some years later were to become notorious as "the Gang of Four", were then exerting considerable sway in the government. Because of Jiang Qing's close association with her ageing and enfeebled husband they were influencing some of its policies in directions different from Zhou's ideas. He no doubt intended his remark to be not only lodged firmly in the civil servants' minds, but also passed on by them to other important officials who might be wondering whether the group's influence was going to prevail against his.

In fact Zhou did remain Prime Minister for nearly another five years, until his death at the beginning of 1976. Throughout the last eighteen months of that period, however, he was confined to a hospital, where he received constant treatment for incurable cancer. He did continue doing his official work as Prime Minister through every day there, for he remained in good mental health. But towards the end of that time his doctors would not allow him to see any people other than his beloved wife, some essential Ministerial colleagues and government officials, and unavoidable foreign visitors with whom he must discuss current working problems. And his restriction to a hospital meant that outside it "the Gang of Four" could assert much more influence than they would otherwise have done if he had been free to move around widely in the capital and through the country.

During my visit to Beijing in 1975 I received a very kind message from him expressing great pleasure that I was back in China, and deep sorrow that we could not meet. His doctors had forbidden all non-essential contacts by him as he lay on his deathbed.

12 "The Gang of Four"

FOR A SHORT WHILE AFTER MAO ZEDONG'S DEATH HIS WIDOW AND THE GROUP OF Communist zealots who shared her extreme political views continued to assert great influence in some fields of the government's policies. Wise, up-and-coming Hua Guofeng (Hua Kuo-feng), who several months earlier had succeeded Zhou Enlai as Premier, now also succeeded Mao as the Party Chairman. But in the then existing circumstances he had to conduct himself with political caution, seeming perhaps to be ready to collaborate with those ultra-leftists. As I have indicated, their grip on affairs had been tightening for some time, especially after Zhou was confined to hospital. This was partly because during Mao's declining years the fanatical trait in his political outlook tended, with Jiang Qing's encouragement, to predominate over the more responsible element which, partly because of Zhou's influence, had usually prevailed through the long years of his prime.

It was true that the more extremist trait had occasionally played a strong part in Mao's shaping of events in those mellow years. It had sparked off, for instance, the deplorable excesses as well as the admirable developments which occurred during the Cultural Revolution. Some of the features of that explosive episode were very good, such as the instruction of virtually the entire populace in the Thoughts of Chairman Mao which, among other results, persuaded the whole people, old and young, male and female alike, to practise the excellent ethical code of personal conduct which the *Little Red Book* advocated. This continued to be just about universally followed by them for several years afterwards.

Other features of the Cultural Revolution, however, were bad, producing almost disastrous results. I have described how one of these was the closing of all the schools, colleges and universities in the urban areas, and the intrusion of cohorts of young Red Guards into the party offices, factories and other places to engage in revolutionary activities such as the expulsions of "capitalist roaders" and other alleged reactionaries from executive committees and similar bodies everywhere. As a result of the licence given to those troupes of keen but immature and sometimes very undisciplined youngsters many of the pragmatically and wisely responsible authorities in, for example, important industrial projects were banished, with crippling consequences such as reductions of production in many factories and the complete closure of others. I need not expand again on those calamitous events, and will simply emphasize that "the Gang of Four" were largely responsible for their occurrence.

Only after long and often frustratingly difficult efforts did Zhou Enlai and his more moderate supporters manage to pull the nation back from the edge of a precipice, and to save the People's Republic from a disastrous collapse. Nevertheless, some of the unhappy consequences of the episode persisted. The decline, and indeed retrogression, in the development of the nation's economy could not be checked and reversed overnight, nor in a short period of time. But after a while the revival began. This was

Children of all ages seem delighted to dance and even the youngest are not in the least self-conscious at this Beijing Commune

partly because of Zhou's reinstatement in office of some of the experienced and able individuals who had been dismissed at the height of the Cultural Revolution. Gradually, with the help of the re-appointed officials, progress in the nation's development began to be in some ways re-established. The country's nation-wide agricultural and industrial advance was resumed, and the prospect of fresh improvements in the well-being of the people appeared promising.

Then the next blow struck the state. Chou Enlai fell ill, and could only do such governmental work as was possible from a hospital ward. Jiang Qing and her ultra-left comrades were able to assert wider influence. They maintained some of the more unfortunate policies instituted during the Cultural Revolution. For example, the reader will recall that one of the matters which Zhou Enlai and Chen Yi mentioned to me in 1962 was that during the Great Leap Forward some of their colleagues had expected that a fully egalitarian Communist society could be established very quickly, in which everyone would be unselfishly dedicated to the service of their fellow-countrymen and

Acrobatic performers train from an early age. These balancing acts are by the Shanghai Circus and Guilin Junior Acrobatic Troupe

would work hard without any wish to receive extra material rewards for themselves on account of especially fine labour. Those over-optimists had at that time learned that this was a mistaken judgement of human nature, that most people would work harder and better only if they were offered material incentives for doing so, and that therefore the move towards a model egalitarian society must be a slow step-by-step process. For this reason higher pay had continued to be given to workers and peasants who laboured more productively than their comrades, privately owned plots of land were restored to every peasant family in hitherto wholly collectively-owned agricultural communes, and some other inducements were given.

During the Cultural Revolution "the Gang of Four" had jogged this policy backwards. Generally in the communes, for instance, they abolished the incentive of higher pay for harder work by the peasants. In them they also withdrew the village production teams' freedom to make decisions on certain plannings of their commune's crops programmes, and restored complete bureaucratic control in local and regional as well as national agricultural policy to the Party's cadres. It was as a consequence of these changes that a partial slowing-down in the pace of advance towards the attainment of very ambitious agricultural production targets did occur. Similar shifts of policy were introduced into industrial affairs, with similar results.

Such policies were criticized by many of the professionally well-trained and practically experienced Ministers, civil servants and other officials in the central, provincial, county and municipal administrations, although they were supported by many others, including of course the more extremist types who got installed in posts during the Cultural Revolution. Disagreement with "the Gang of Four's" attitudes was not allowed, and this was the reason why literally thousands of dissidents had then been expelled from their offices. Many of these experienced and sagacious individuals were banished to remote rural areas where they were forced to spend all their working hours tending pigs or engaging in other such farmyard labour in communes. The expulsion of their knowledgeable brains from the conduct of policies in central Ministries, municipal councils and other governmental bodies was a terrible, widespread loss to the nation. As I have mentioned, after a while Zhou Enlai had been able to reinstate some of them in office, but only a small minority of them. After his death "the Gang" re-expelled some of these, one of them being again Deng Siaoping. As a result the economic, social and political advance of the seriously under-developed nation was checked again.

Moreover, this backsliding threatened to become continuous as a result of the regime's policy regarding education in schools, colleges and universities. I wrote earlier that when those institutions of learning were reopened after a considerable period of closure in the cities and towns during the Cultural Revolution the type of teaching in them – and in schools throughout the countrysides as well – was in certain ways radically altered. Communist ideology was given more importance as a subject for study in pupils' classrooms than were scholastic matters; the number of years spent by teenagers in middle schools was substantially reduced; no youngsters went straight from schools to universities for higher learning, all of them being sent instead to toil for two or three years as workers in industrial factories or peasants in agricultural communes; and the examination system for their subsequent entry into a university was abolished.

I have also already written that when I was in China in 1971 I was told that these changes in the educational system were "experimental"; their results would be carefully

Beijing Opera Star, Li Bingshu

A scene from The Women Generals of the Yang Family *by the Shanghai-Beijing Opera Company*

Opposite : An actor from the Changsha Opera

observed, and they might be modified later. Evidently certain people in high places felt very dubious about them. I expect that this was one of the matters on which Zhou Enlai held a different view from Jiang Qing and her adherents, and that he planned that the government would revert, in some ways at least, to earlier practices when the faults of the existing system became obvious. However, no modification had been introduced before his influence waned very seriously, and the policy was maintained as long as "the Gang" stayed in power.

The closing of schools, colleges and universities during the Cultural Revolution of course meant that through that period the members of the school-age and university-age generation in the urban areas received no scholastic education whatever; and the change in the curriculum after their reopening meant that the youngsters everywhere continued to be to a considerable extent deprived of that type of learning. This also meant that their teachers, lecturers and professors were unable to practise adequately their own academic skills, with a consequent fall-off in their abilities. In addition it meant that the training of not only new youthful academics but also other young professional people of various types was distinctly less thorough and good. So by the late 1970s a ten years gap had occurred in the production of properly tutored and trained experts in several important fields of national activity. Through no fault of their own their specialist qualifications to do their jobs had fallen distinctly below what they should have been, with unhappy consequences for the nation's progress.

"The Gang" maintained other policies also which, in their view, would help to make the People's Republic of China an unassailable Communist state free from any risk of corruption by Imperialist, capitalist or other evil influences. They continued, for instance, to forbid lovely theatrical performances of classical Chinese operas in which actors and actresses dressed in fabulous costumes of the Song, Ming or Qing Dynasties sang and danced romantic scenes reminiscent of those old times. No audience was permitted to become acquainted with, and still less to be enchanted by, beautiful representations of the oppressive feudal ages. Large crowds of workers and peasants did still flock to theatres to enjoy operas and ballets, but the only dramas that they could witness represented heroic military or other deeds recently enacted by members of the People's Red Army, the Red Guards or other Communist troupes in new China.

For the same propagandist reason contacts with other kinds of non-Communist cultures were now prohibited. Whereas, for instance, in earlier post-1949 years famous symphony orchestras of musicians from European countries had been periodically invited to come to play concerts of the works of Bach, Beethoven, Mozart and other noble composers to enthusiastic audiences in Beijing, Shanghai, Guangzhou and other populous cities in China, no such invitations were issued during the later period of rule by "the Gang of Four" after Zhou fell gravely ill. Nor could the Chinese acquire books written by literary geniuses such as Charles Dickens, Alexandre Dumas, Leo Tolstoy or other non-Maoist authors. The authorities in Beijing sought to cut off almost completely any communication between their people and the peoples of the "reactionary" outside world. So the Chinese population was kept more or less isolated from the rest of mankind – almost as it had been through much of the old feudal era when the Emperors and their mandarins regarded the Chinese as the only civilized people on Earth, whilst all other peoples were contemptible "foreign devils" and "barbarians".

13 China Now

THE MORE SENSIBLE LEADERS OF THE BY NATURE SENSIBLE CHINESE PEOPLE WHO STILL retained some authority in the government disagreed with the fanatical policies being pursued by the political extremists. They were aware of the damaging effects which these were having on the nation's hoped-for steadily increasing economic and social development. Very soon after Mao's death, in October 1976, they succeeded in ousting "the Gang of Four" from power.

Chairman Hua played a quietly influential part in the lead-up to their removal, and then ordered their arrest and confinement. He has continued ever since to be both the Chairman of the Party and the Premier in the State Council. His shrewd judgements in the formulation and conduct of policies have had distinct influence in initiating the nation's recovery which is now under way. One of his and his supporters' early decisions was to recall to important governmental posts many of the experienced administrators and other experts who had previously been dismissed. Among others Deng Xiaoping was again brought back from exile, and became the principal Vice-Premier in the State Council. Those two statesmen form an admirable partnership, and they are greatly helped by a team of capable colleagues, many of whom had also been deprived of office through the recent years.

Indeed, since the change thousands of the talented civil servants, economists, academics and other experts who had earlier been dismissed from their jobs because of their disagreements with "the Gang's" policies have been brought back from the tending of pigs or other manual labours in rural areas, to resume their professional work. Some of them had suffered psychological or other ailments which damaged their capacities, but most of them immediately became once more their old experienced and able selves. Their qualities were badly needed in immense quantities to help in restoring the nation's economic, social and other sorts of progress.

Nevertheless, owing to the almost ten years gap in the scholarly, professional or technical training of such individuals their numbers were in very short supply. The proper tuition of many new ones was urgently needed. To achieve this a return to some of the earlier methods of youngsters' schooling and higher education was required, such as the re-introduction of the right scholarly subjects for teaching in classrooms, the admission of qualified youngsters to universities immediately after they left middle schools (instead of them having to go to do two or three years manual work in factories or communes in the meantime), and the restoration of the examination system in colleges so that the best intellectually qualified people would be selected for important administrative and related posts. These restorations were some of the early acts of the new government.

Crowds waiting outside the Chairman Mao mausoleum and portraits of him over doorways in the Forbidden City

The Chairman's and Ministers' principal aim was of course to re-establish as firm and quick an advance as was practicable in China's modern development, which would give its population increasing well-being. The means of achieving this was by restimulating a steady transformation of its economy from a still considerably out-of-date state of affairs to a completely up-to-date one. To succeed in performing that colossal task the nation's security must also be ensured. For these purposes the authorities in Beijing proclaimed that their policy would be the progressive attainment of China's modernization in the four spheres earlier declared by Zhou Enlai to be of supreme importance – agriculture, industry, defence and·scientific technology.

They stated that to succeed in practice the Chinese must be realists. They must not make the mistake of over-optimism about the pace at which their ultimate goals could be reached which some of the leaders had committed during the Great Leap Forward. Progress could not be rapid: the immense effort would take time – a great deal of time. A comprehensive development on a country-wide scale of their considerable mineral resources, of all the numerous essential types of both light and heavy industries, and of a much more thoroughly irrigated, richly fertilized and adequately mechanized agriculture could not be attained overnight, or even in a few years. If properly planned, the advance could be steady, but only gradual. The leaders reckoned that the process of modernization in every necessary way could only be completely achieved by about the end of the Twentieth Century, or even a while later. They coined the phrase that the Chinese were now engaged on "a new Long March".

They recognized that if they were going to succeed in reaching their goals they must have the keen co-operation of the whole population toiling energetically in mines, factories and fields. They also recognized that to gain this they must restore some of the encouraging practices which "the Gang of Four" had abolished or restricted. They therefore re-introduced various kinds of material incentives for hard labour by the masses, including the award of higher pay for more productive efforts by peasants and workers. Nor were these the only types of individuals who again received more material rewards for devoted work. The "national capitalists" were given back some of the properties of which they had been deprived during the Cultural Revolution, or compensation for those which could not be returned.

The new leaders also thought that, with a view to not simply maintaining but also increasing ever more eager working support from the labouring multitudes, those people should have rather more say in influencing policies than they had been permitted during the last several years. They reckoned that "the Gang" had been wrong to concentrate autocratic power in the hands of government bureaucrats in the conduct at every level of the nation's activities. In their view the ordinary folk should be consulted much more regarding the means of implementing locally the over-all, centrally settled agricultural and industrial policies. They therefore returned considerably more autonomy in the making of decisions on local production plans and related matters to village teams in the communes and to workshop teams in the factories. This did increase those people's constructive co-operation in carrying out the projects decided by the supreme authorities.

In another important, broader way they sought to encourage that kind of co-operation. They started to give the ordinary citizens more freedom to express their opinions, and perhaps to influence policies, in national political as well as local economic affairs. For example, the publication and circulation of independently written pamphlets and magazines was permitted. The most famous way in which members of the general public were allowed to propagate their ideas was by pasting posters which everyone could read on what became known as the "Democracy Wall" in the centre of Beijing. Various individuals and groups – supporters and critics of the government alike – could publicize their views by sticking large written placards there expressing agreement or disagreement with this or that aspect of official activities. I shall return to that subject later.

In political matters another development was important as a step towards more democracy. Whereas the People's National Congress had hitherto met very rarely – only about half-a-dozen times for brief periods during the last thirty years – it and its standing committee now began to hold much more regular sessions for discussions of policy and the passage of legislation. So the executive Ministers in the State Council came into quite frequent contact with those indirectly elected representatives of the people.

All these developments were results of some freedom of rethinking in which leaders in the government themselves were engaging. Several of them were not critics solely of "the Gang of Four": they felt sceptical even about parts of the teachings of the great Revolutionary prophet Mao Zedung himself. They did not question the wisdom of his supreme Communist beliefs; on this they continued to be among his devoted disciples. Nor did they disagree with the rightness of other lofty principles which he had preached concerning human public affairs and private behaviour. What they questioned, and indeed sometimes disagreed with, were certain of the methods which he advocated for achieving some of those noble principles in practice, including the means by which a completely Communist society could in due course be established. They judged that he had been in some ways too extremist in his outlook, attempting to reach his ultimate aims by wrong or too hasty methods. He was too much of a theoretical idealist, and not enough of a practical realist.

That thought got expressed in some Communist Party discussions in 1978 when it was affirmed that "Practice is the sole criterion for testing truth" – not theoretical notions written in ideological textbooks, however correct the main theses presented in such literary works might be. And the authors of this declaration urged that some of Mao's practices had definitely proved mistaken, such as the excessive speed of the industrial development planned during the Great Leap Forward and the extremist political dogmatism imposed during the Cultural Revolution. Indeed, they thought that the launching of the Cultural Revolution itself had been a grave error; and they rejected Mao's idea that similar Revolutions must take place periodically over the years. They indicated that there should be no more Cultural Revolutions.

I repeat that the new Ministers were still dedicated supporters of Mao's principal doctrines. They continued to pay homage to him as a very great leader. But they recognized that he was a mortal Man, not a divine God. Like all great men, he had his faults as well as his superb qualities. He could occasionally make mistakes.

At a succession of meetings of influential government and party bodies through 1978 and early 1979 the new leaders and their advisers engaged in a tense re-examination and reappraisal of the current situation and the future prospects regarding China's economic development. The expert professional economists who had been expelled from office in previous years, and were now reinstated, played an eminent part in analysing the errors

Overleaf: The Square of Heavenly Peace, Beijing

171

that had been made in the past and in deciding what changes must be introduced in this crucially important field of policy. It was agreed that there had been a considerable over-expansion of the capital construction programme aiming at an impossibly swift comprehensive nation-wide advance throughout mining, agriculture and industry. Capital investment plans would now have to be scaled down, and errors which had been made in selecting priorities for development must be corrected. A careful reassessment must be made of the right order of precedences for this or that type of mining, agricultural, and light, medium or heavy industrial productions. It was also agreed that some errors had been made earlier about the proper geographical areas where certain kinds of farm crops should be grown. It had been wrong, for instance, to seek to promote rice-growing in the climatically unsuitable north instead of keeping it confined to, and expanded in, the more tropical southern regions. I must not attempt to go into details about the various contemplated revisions.

The authorities decided that the years 1979–81 would be a period of "readjustment, restructuring, consolidation and improvement" with a view to launching the proper fresh gradual yet massive advance.

As part of the process the Ministers did some rethinking in another matter of significance. It was true that, in spite of the periodic setbacks, the development of the national economy through the last almost thirty years had grown on an impressive scale, and that because of an immense, unprecedented production of oil and other mineral resources, a country-wide expansion and improvement in the cultivation of many sorts of agricultural crops, and the considerable increases in the output of often novel industrial products China had become much more self-reliant in providing its people's needs than it used to be. The extent of the quite formidable progress is illustrated by the following statistics, which show the quantities of certain important, representative mining, agricultural and industrial outputs produced in 1949, 1952 (the year preceding the start of the first five-years plan) and 1978 respectively:

	1949	1952	1978
Crude oil	121,000 tons	436,000	104,050,000
Coal	32,430,000 tons	66,490,000	618,000,000
Grain	113,200,000 tons	163,900,000	304,750,000
Sugar cane	2,642,000 tons	7,116,000	21,117,000
Hogs	57,750,000 hogs	89,770,000	301,290,000
Steel	158,000 tons	1,349,000	31,780,000
Cotton cloth	1,890,000 metres	3,830,000	11,029,000

The figures for the extensions of transport routes in those same years are as follows:

	1949	1952	1978
Motor roads	80,700 kilometres	126,000	890,000
Railways	22,000 kilometres	24,500	50,400
Inland waterways	73,600 kilometres	95,000	136,000

Nevertheless the Ministers in Beijing recognized that if further progress was to be made reasonably quickly in adequate ways, the Chinese could not be so self-reliant as had previously been supposed. A great deal more help would be required from the

Street cobblers in Beijing and card players in Guangzhou

Above : An elderly Chinese walks past a poster in Shanghai
Below : A crowd around new notices on 'Democracy Wall' in Beijing

outside world than had been foreseen and planned earlier. In particular they needed to be supplied by some of the much more modernly developed nations with sophisticated technological know-how and equipments. The reader will remember that Zhou Enlai spoke to me about this need in one of my talks with him: but perhaps even he did not realize to what an extent it would become essential. In the emotional aftermath of the withdrawal of Russian aid he may have judged that China could be more self-reliant than was really practicable, at any rate at this stage of its advance.

The new team now became fully aware of the fact, and so became more outward looking in the pursuit of their aims of modernization in the national economy and defence than their predecessors had been. Certain difficulties existed regarding the problem. For example, owing to China's considerable isolation from overseas nations in both the rather distant and the very recent past it possessed insufficient foreign exchange for helping to make the huge purchases of many technological and other materials which it now wished to buy from some of them. This could continue to slow down seriously the pace of its advance. To help in overcoming the difficulties the Ministers in Beijing revised in certain ways policies which their predecessors had very strictly adhered to. One example of this was their resolve to earn quite a lot more of various foreign currencies by selling in overseas markets many of the artistic treasures of which large numbers had been excavated in the last three decades, and any exports at all of which had hitherto been prohibited. Another reversal of an earlier policy was their decision to negotiate agreements for large financial loans from overseas banks, an action which the Chinese authorities had hitherto always refused to contemplate. And they also decided to invite foreign business firms to co-operate with Chinese state bodies in carrying out joint industrial and other projects in China.

I made my most recent visit to China in March 1979, when I led a small group of officers of the Great Britain–China Centre on some travels there. Through the last several years the wisely forward-looking Centre has helped to promote mutually advantageous exchanges and co-operation between the two countries in various professional and cultural fields. Our very kind hosts during our fortnight in China were the Chinese People's Association for Friendship with Foreign Countries.

One of the features of changing China which I observed was of course the Democracy Wall in Beijing. It was covered with written posters, some of them criticizing certain aspects of the government's policies and others retorting with statements in their defence. It was rather like a kind of House of Assembly where written, not spoken, debates about national affairs could take place freely. The audience of observers who stood around reading the arguments and counter-arguments did occasionally contribute little speeches of agreement or disagreement with this or that written contention.

In recent times some of the placards had been rather vehemently hostile to the government's attitude on matters of great importance. After a while the authorities made it clear that although such criticisms could continue within certain limits, they must not go beyond those limits. The fundamental tenets of the Communist faith, for instance, must not be derided. Some of the more virulent posters got pulled down from the Wall, and certain of their authors were arrested and expelled to a region where they could not continue those activities.

177

Above : The Jade Buddha in the temple of that name, Shanghai

Opposite : Beijing Mosque and the Altar of the Roman Catholic Cathedral

I observed other bits of evidence of the degree of freedom of thought and speech which the people were now allowed. In private conversations with many individuals their talk had become even more relaxed than it was with some of them four years ago. Their comments on affairs were more originally instead of officially phrased, and they were quite often especially critical of the conduct of government bureaucrats. The speakers evidently felt distinctly more inclined and able to state their own personal opinions on various topics than had been the case a few years earlier. Nevertheless, certain current Party slogans quite often got repeated again and again by people wherever one went, in urban and rural areas alike. What was significant was that the slogans had on certain matters changed. No one any longer blamed the old "capitalist roaders" for whatever unhappy contemporary conditions a person was describing. Everyone declared that "the Gang of Four" were the guilty party.

In that connection another remark made by a scholarly man guiding my travelling companions and me round the ancient Summer Palace of Changde, which had been built during the reign of the Emperor K'ang Hsi for his and his successors' resort during the hot months of each year, was interesting. As we were about to enter one of the beautiful Pavilions there he pointed to a decorative piece of calligraphy carved and gilded on a wooden panel above its doorway, and he said with evident admiration, "That was designed by the Emperor Ch'ien Lung". Clearly His Imperial Majesty was no longer regarded simply as a wicked reactionary tyrant, but also as a talented patron and promoter of Chinese art. Incidentally, that Pavilion and the other regal buildings scattered across a spacious lakeside park were being restored to their original forms, so that crowds of Chinese visitors and foreign tourists would be able to enjoy their Qing Dynasty architectural beauty when that repair work was finished and the site could be opened to the public.

Another sign of the re-awakening of an appreciation of the fine creations of past eras was the restoration of performances of classical dramas on theatrical stages. In one city our hospitable hosts took us to watch an ancient Chinese opera being acted by a troupe of actors and actresses brilliantly dressed in fabulous costumes of a feudal age. The vast auditorium was filled with a multitude of Chinese people, who clapped enthusiastically in delight at the scenes. In another city our hosts took us to a theatre where another team of actors and actresses were singing and stepping antique Chinese folk-songs and country dances. Again the place was filled with an eagerly watching, listening and often applauding audience of the local people. Of course, now and then – but much less frequently than before – the new Revolutionary operas and ballets were also being performed. The two epochs of Chinese culture were being reunited.

At the same time the concept of modern society which everyone was taught, and almost always fully accepted, was a Communist one. In the communes' villages and the factories' workshops all the peasants and workers were still indoctrinated in the Marxist–Leninist–Maoist political philosophy. But this subject did not monopolize all the time in all their educative discussion groups, as it used to do. During them the people were being taught other lessons too, such as technological sciences helpful to their industrial or agricultural activities, and foreign languages such as English and Japanese.

The partial setback to the growth of the national economy which had resulted from the policies of "the Gang of Four" was starting to be reversed. At the time of my visit, however, this resumed progress had not yet been sufficient to allow a further rise in the population's standard of living above the pre-"Gang of Four" period level. Nevertheless the outlook was promising, and I saw various signs of other improvements since my stay in the country in 1975. For instance, there was, again a considerably greater variety of attractive goods made in China for sale in the shops, such as a wider assortment of children's toys. The same was true regarding articles of clothing for men, women and youngsters alike – and among the more decorative dresses for females were, at last, a few charmingly adorned cheongsam-type garments.

Nor were young women now only anxious to wear rather decorative dresses. They were beginning to care, and to take trouble, about other aspects of their appearances. A few years ago their hair-dos had been largely uniform, consisting of straight-cut, flatly-brushed short locks hanging only as low as the tops of their necks. Now many of the females of various ages were having their hair artificially curled and coiffed in fanciful styles. A desire to use lipstick and other cosmetics seemed to be hovering in the air.

Brisk trade in thermos flasks at No. One Department Store Shanghai, essential for hot water to replenish the innumerable cups of tea, and the toy counter in Chaoyang Commune Store, Shanghai

Other signs of advancing change appeared in the cities' streets. Many more small motor cars, large freight vehicles and buses sped along the highways. They were all still publicly owned. Although perhaps by now a few individuals could afford to buy a car, no-one was allowed to own privately even a tiny mini-car. But there was a vast increase in the numbers of bicycles being pedalled around. At certain hours of the day multitudes of them hastened on the roads, like torrents of rushing water pouring along a flooded river. I was told that in Beijing about 3,000,000 push-bikes were now owned by its citizens, and that in Shanghai there were about 4,000,000 of them.

The amount of traffic on the country roads had also distinctly increased since four years earlier. There were many more motor vehicles and pedalled bicycles as well as animal- or human-drawn carts on the move everywhere. One reason for some of this was one of the material incentives recently re-introduced by the government into commune life to encourage hard labour by the peasants in agricultural production. It had restored the villagers' right to sell vegetables, eggs and animals grown, layed or bred on their private plots of ground. So wherever my colleagues and I journeyed in rural areas we saw many, many peasants taking heaps of those foodstuffs, loaded in carts or packed on the carriers of their bicycles, to open-air markets in near-by small towns, where crowds of customers were purchasing them. The only restriction imposed on the sellers was that they must not charge more than the current fixed prices for the articles concerned. They could charge less if they wanted to.

Another cause of the increased traffic crowding the urban and rural areas was very important. It was the growth of the population. In spite of the people's on the whole loyal acceptance of the policy of family planning their numbers were quite rapidly increasing – partly because of the steadily improving health services. Their total number now exceeded 950,000,000, most of them being younger than middle-age. This was one reason why there had been no recent appreciable rise in their material standard of living, since it was difficult for the increasing production of consumer goods by agriculture and industry to keep pace with the growing multitudes of their consumers.

Indeed, the hugely growing population is perhaps China's principal problem. The authorities judged that a more serious attempt must be made to reduce its rate of increase. I learned of a rather astonishing consequence of this attitude. When my companions and I visited the most abundantly populated Province in the country, Sichuan (Szechuan), where about 100,000,000 people lived, we were told that a few days earlier a revised family planning policy had been launched by the Provincial authorities. Whereas previously all married couples had been encouraged to confine the number of their children to two, that number was now reduced to one. The means of persuading them to do this was as follows. If a newly wedded couple undertook to have only one offspring, when that infant was born they received an extra 5 yuan a month to help in its upkeep, schooling and other needs. If later "by accident" or for some other reason a second youngster was born to them, not only would they receive no such payments for the newcomer but also no further payments would be made for their first-born.

I understand that this scheme has now become a national policy covering all the

Opposite top : A bicycle park in Beijing

Opposite bottom : A stairway for pedestrians with a special bicycle track over a bridge on the Pearl River, Guangzhou

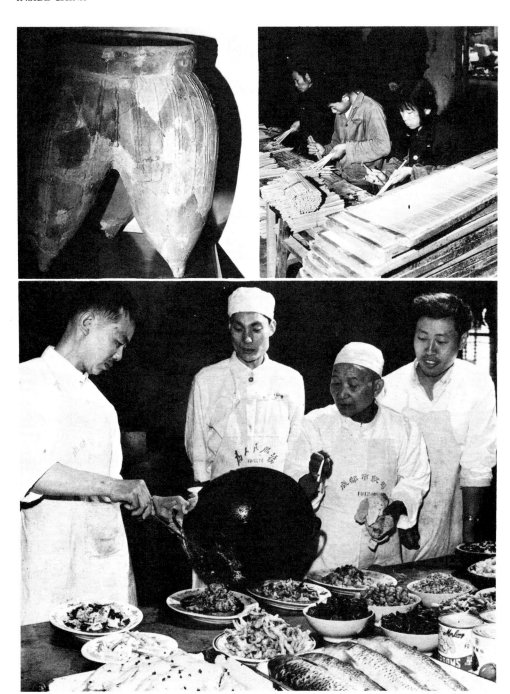

The preparation and presentation of food have always been an important art. The three-legged pot enabled three dishes to be cooked at once. Chopsticks are made at the Arts and Crafts Centre, Guilin and a master chef demonstrates Sichuan (Szechwan) cooking. Opposite, a crane carved from vegetables decorates a dish in the famous Beijing Roast Duck Restaurant

Provinces. The authorities are hoping that the rate of increase of the country's population can be reduced to less than 1% per annum.

Nevertheless, the minority nationalities are still exempted from any family planning efforts.

Accompanied by my travelling companions I had the great privilege of discussing the contemporary situation with Vice-Premier Deng Ziaoping in Beijing. His outstanding ability and dynamic forcefulness gleamed brightly in every sentence that he spoke. One indication of his resolute character was that he never wasted a word. Every phrase that he uttered added something positively informative about whatever subject we were considering.

He emphasized that the government's top aim was the achievement of modernization in the nation's agriculture, industry, defence and scientific technology by the end of the present century. He added that even if that goal was reached by then, there would still be a wide gap between China and the developed Western countries in such matters as the "per capita" incomes of their populations. The material standard of living of the Chinese people would for a considerable time continue to be lower than that of most of the European and the North American peoples. This was partly because of the very backward state of the national economy and of the nation's defence equipment from which modernization still had to spring, and which made it necessary to give a higher priority to the expenditure of large sums of money to other, capital fields of development than to speedy rises in the people's family incomes. Another reason was the huge size of the Chinese population, which amounted to nearly a quarter of the total population of the world. Their material standard of living could not catch up with that of the Western peoples until some time in the next century.

Deng said that owing to their lack of earlier experience in vital development fields, modernization was proving more difficult than many of the Chinese leaders had at first thought. And the incompetent tackling of problems, including the lack of proper training of new professional and technical experts, during the years of rule by "the Gang of Four" had slowed the whole process. The level of Chinese technology now, at the end of the 1970s, was roughly that which the European nations had attained in the 1950s. If things progressed well, in a great majority of fields China should be approaching the current Western level by about the year 2000; but in some cases it would still be falling behind, whilst in one or two others it might perhaps be overtaking the West.

Reasonably speedy success depended partly on the Chinese being able to learn from up-to-date Western experience and skills, which required the import of a lot of technology and capital equipment from advanced countries overseas. Much would of course also depend on the Chinese people's ability to absorb into their economy, manage competently and further improve everything that was so introduced. He personally felt confidence in their capacity as well as determination to do this well.

On political affairs, when I asked Deng whether the present Chinese government felt that it had perhaps been trying in present circumstances to go "too far too fast" in intro-

Opposite and overleaf: The Chinese view of their own achievements in industry. Engineers work on power lines across the Yellow River

Below : Reservoirs along the Dadu river facilitate timber collecting and transporting. Motor boats haul the timber rafts

Opposite top : A drilling team at Shengli Oilfield and ingots being poured in a steel factory in Hunan Province

Opposite bottom : Cultivation by animals has been largely superseded by locally constructed tractors such as these in Guangxi Zhuang Region

ducing considerably more democratic practices into the state, he nodded his head. He then said that the constitution of the People's Republic of China described the practice of its government as "democratic centralism". This meant that, whilst being based on the will of the people, the central government exercised a great deal of authoritative power in devising and enacting the policies desired by those people. But in the past several years there had been too much centralism and not enough democracy. The present government was therefore liberalizing the political system. However, every new situation, every step forward, created its own fresh problems. Regarding the introduction of more democracy, such problems had already appeared and were no surprise. They had been anticipated, and would now be dealt with.

He emphasized that there must be more freedom of speech, including criticism, than the government had allowed in earlier times. But the criticisms should be constructive and helpful, not destructive. They should not be allowed to weaken, and still less to destroy the nation's supremely important programme of progressive modernization.

Some of them, such as certain of the posters pasted on the Democracy Wall, were threatening to do that. They sought to promote indiscipline among young people which could obstruct the aims of the government and population as a whole. Other of the criticisms were presented in a different spirit; they sought to assist the government in guiding the national policies in wise ways which would maintain and increase the people's keen support. That was the purpose of democratic centralization, which should create a co-operative partnership between the leaders and the masses of their fellow countrymen.

Guilin airport set against eroded mountains, which often feature in Chinese art

Deng commented that nothing that had happened meant that the development of democracy should be curbed. But the criticisms that it allowed should of course be kept within the law. There was need to strengthen the legal system so that the law in all matters was firmly enforced. And an extremely important additional need was that the members of the young generation should be educated about the necessity for the laws, and about the sensible reasons why, in the interests of the whole community, they should be friendlily obeyed.

In the course of our talk Deng remarked that in all societies there were not only political counter-revolutionaries but also "social dregs". Some social dregs in China were now making it hard to maintain social order. They were not simply expressing wild ideas but also performing wicked acts. A dozen years ago ethical standards and moral conduct throughout the country were very good: but since then there had been some deterioration. For example, prostitutes "under another guise" had recently appeared, for the first time since 1949. Some other ancient vices too were beginning to raise their ugly heads again in the conduct of individuals who were inclined to indulge in crimes.

I must express my personal opinion that this relapse in ethical standards, like some of the other changes which were taking place, was natural. It would have occurred inevitably sooner or later in one way or another. The honeymoon period of the Revolution was over; the very emotional, unquestioning devotion of the masses of liberated people to all the Thoughts of Mao was coming to an end. All those individuals were returning to more normal ways of thinking and acting. The Chinese are typical human beings, endowed with the weaknesses as well as the strengths of mortal men and women. They are blessed with noble virtues which enable them to create superb achievements in many civilized spheres; but also inborn in them are less good traits which can make them indulge in all sorts of sins. As much as any race of people round the world they are of this Earth earthy.

Their extremely difficult population problem contributes to their present social difficulties. Whereas in the early years of the nation's economic development none of the already hundreds of millions of adult Chinese were unemployed because that progress was being achieved very largely by their manual labour, in the later years the expansion has been done to an increasing extent with the aid of productive machines. So it is becoming increasingly difficult year by year for many young school leavers to find jobs when they come on to the labour market. They become unemployed. As happens in other countries where that situation exists, many of these frustrated individuals are tempted to turn to mischievous occupations. Hence the recent increases in resort to various kinds of crimes in China. In other cases such youngsters turn to good activities. They try to consider reasonably what is the cause of their unfortunate state of affairs, and some at least of them decide that the nation's governing authorities must be partly responsible for it. They feel critical of their leaders' policies, wish to express freely their opinions – and robust arguments break out.

At the present period the tendency for both those sorts of consequences to occur is growing quite strong in China. As I indicated in an earlier chapter, so long as an overwhelming majority of the grown-up people there belonged to the generations who recalled their miserable conditions of living before 1949 they were naturally extremely grateful to Mao Zedung and his colleagues who had improved their circumstances almost beyond recognition. So the population was devotedly loyal to their government. But now that most of the people cannot personally remember those past conditions, they are less satisfied with their present still rather simple way of life. And they learn through the modern news media about the much better material conditions in which the people of many other lands live. So they compare their present lot not with that of their parents or grandparents thirty years ago, but with that of the Americans, the Japanese, the Europeans and others in contemporary times. And they feel some discontent. Numbers of them become rebels in one way or another.

In that connection, through the latter months of 1979 some of the posters stuck on the Democracy Wall in Beijing attacked certain government policies with a viciousness which the authorities judged to be dangerously harmful to continuing law-abiding national unity. Towards the end of the year the right to conduct propaganda there, in the populous centre of the capital, was withdrawn. It is still permitted elsewhere in the city, but in a less popular gathering place.

The overwhelming majority of the Chinese people are evidently at present satisfied with their new leaders' policies, partly because of the reforms in them, and partly because of their further promises. One of my unforgettably pleasing impressions during my latest travels in China was the look on the faces of the people wherever I went. In the cities, towns, villages and countrysides alike they all looked healthy, happy and self-confident. In conversation they showed a strong, dedicated determination to help their leaders to carry through in practice their ambitious plans for China's advance. Many of them spoke of "the new Long March" on which the nation has begun.

14 China in the World

AT THE TIME OF MY VISIT IN MARCH 1979 CHINA'S INTERNATIONAL RELATIONS WERE passing through a significant stage. One reason for this was its Ministers' recognition that their plans for the nation's economic development required very good trading relations with some highly sophisticated industrial foreign states. This made them anxious to establish several such friendly co-operative associations.

The only modernized state from which they wanted no such help was Russia. This was partly because they felt that they could not trust that help. When they had earlier been assured of it, and had indeed received it in valuable ways for a few years, the Russians suddenly withheld it without prior warning, causing very serious relapses in their further development plans. Another reason for their attitude was their conviction that the rulers in the Kremlin desired to spread Russian "hegemony" into every corner of the world, and that any assistance that they gave would be designed primarily to serve that purpose. Consequently the Chinese government now refused to renew on the existing terms the Treaty of Friendship with the Soviet Union which had been signed by a previous government of the People's Republic, and which would soon be due for re-signing. Instead they proposed that a fresh series of talks should start between the two governments in an attempt to remove the outstanding disagreements existing between them on their frontier problem and other questions. Relations between the two principal Communist countries had slipped from being cool to becoming cold.

China's relations with two other important countries which had previously been cool were warming up. The Chinese leaders' earlier suspicions of America's and Japan's hostile intentions towards the People's Republic had been removed. For some years already Japan and China had established diplomatic relations with one another. Now as a result of gradually growing mutual understanding between the American and the Chinese governments they too, at the beginning of 1979, each appointed an

Ambassador in the other's capital. The Americans ceased their earlier obstinate recognition of the regime in Taiwan. Moreover, in treaties of friendship which the Americans and the Japanese respectively signed with the Chinese firm opposition to international "hegemony" by any one power was expressed – a clear indication of those two other nations' accord with China's apprehension regarding the Russians' ambition. This did, of course, represent the attitude of the Americans and the Japanese, and it was evidence of the importance that they attached to China as an increasingly strong influence in countering the Soviet's influence.

Related to the political character of these moves was their economic purpose. The government of poorly under-developed China wanted a lot of practical help from richly developed America and Japan in its plans for the modernization of its agriculture,

Vice Premier Deng Xiaoping greets Malcolm MacDonald in Beijing

industry and other paramount needs. Active trade between China and Japan had been proceeding for several years, but this needed stepping-up. And the Chinese recognized the immense help that they could receive from the technologically extremely advanced Americans, which those previous non-co-operators were now ready to give. Busy contacts to promote these purposes began. Deng Xiaoping paid visits to Washington and Tokyo for discussions on major aspects of mutually beneficial co-operation, and several highly qualified trade delegations went from China to the U.S.A. and to Japan, and from the U.S.A. and Japan to China to make plans. Some useful schemes started to get off the ground.

At the same time the Chinese authorities made similar contacts with Britain and several states in Western Europe to increase as much and as quickly as possible their

Malcolm MacDonald with Chairman Hua Guofeng in London

previous trading co-operation. It was partly to stimulate this, as well as to strengthen mutual political understanding and friendliness, that Chairman Hua Guofeng, accompanied by a large group of fellow Ministers and expert advisers, made working visits to Germany, France, Britain and Italy towards the end of 1979. These produced good results.

So China's development in various important spheres is on the move again. Progress cannot be fast, but it can be steady. The Chinese authorities' ultimate aims are high, but their determination is strong and their resources will grow. And the goodwill of the foreign nations involved is sincere. They recognize the immensely important part which the People's Republic of China can play in helping to guide solutions to international problems in sensible, peaceful ways.

The more congenial relations which have been steadily growing through the last several years between the United States of America and the People's Republic of China have helped to prod the unhappy quarrel between the government of Beijing and the regime in Taiwan towards a possible conciliatory settlement. Deprived of the mighty support of America, as well as of Japan and some other nations, the governors in the latter quite prosperous but small island are having to act cautiously. At the same time the rulers of the progressively strengthening sub-continent just across a strip of sea are acting patiently and prudently, showing an understanding friendship towards the island's people. It is to be hoped that as a result of continuing communications between them the problem can in due course be amicably solved.

The Chinese government's main aim in its foreign policy is to help to ensure that no major war breaks out, so that it can itself continue in undisturbed security to create an ever more thriving and happy Chinese nation. With a view to this it believes sincerely in the principle and practice of peaceful co-existence between all nations, regardless of their different social systems and political ideologies. Perhaps it is still prepared not only to feel moral sympathy with but also occasionally to give material support to "revolutionary" forces fighting against their "oppressors" in other lands; but if that is the case, it would do so in very limited ways which did not threaten to extend the local battle into a wider war. They wish world-wide peace to remain undisturbed.

They see only one threat to that hopeful prospect, and therefore to China's own continuing security and progress. They are convinced that Soviet Russia intends by every possible means to spread ever more widely, first in this region and then in that, its aggressive "hegemony" round the world, until it dominates the whole of humanity. They have kept their eyes and ears open to detect every sign of that ambition, and every now and then they have opened their mouths in efforts to make the rest of mankind aware of the danger. In addition to denouncing the Russians they denounce some smaller Communist states who are acting as "stooges" of their Russian masters, such as the Cubans. And they urge other governments to take appropriate counter actions when necessary against the Russian conspiratorial plan.

Whenever possible the Chinese government itself has taken such action. An example of this had occurred shortly before I arrived in China in mid-March 1979. The brief Chinese military invasion of Vietnam had just taken place, and ended. At its start the Ministers in Beijing announed that it would be a "temporary and punitive" expedition, and that is exactly what it was.

China's relations with the government in Hanoi were among those which had suffered a change during the last few years. As I mentioned earlier, throughout the bitter war which the Vietminh rebels waged against the South Vietnamese and their American and other foreign allies the Chinese, like the Russians, gave material military support to them; and when those northerners gained their eventual complete victory, and assumed power over the whole of Vietnam, good neighbourly relations between China and Vietnam were maintained for a while. The Communist government in Hanoi seemed to favour continuing friendly co-operation with both Communist China and Communist Russia. Later, however, it shifted to the side of Russia against China. The Vietnamese authorities, for instance, refused to hold amicable talks with the Chinese authorities about the small disputed areas along their common land frontier and about some islands off their coasts which each party claimed to be their own territories. The Vietnamese stationed troops along the frontier, and (according to probably correct Chinese accounts) quite often provoked trouble, including shooting incidents.

In other directions also the new Vietnamese government sought to intrude into other peoples' affairs beyond Vietnam's own borders. They had been doing this for some time, in military and other ways, in Laos. Then in February 1979 they made their sudden armed invasion into Cambodia. Many divisions of their army overran that next-door country, forced the admittedly very bad Khmer Rouge government headed by Pol Pot to retreat from Phnom Penh, and installed in its place another Cambodian Communist administration which would be a puppet of the Vietnamese aggressors.

The subsequent "temporary and punitive" invasion of Vietnam by Chinese troops was the Beijing government's reaction to these events. The voluntary withdrawal of those troops which it had foretold took place a few days before I arrived in China.

Above: Chinese soldiers record their visit to Beijing

Overleaf: A fisherman poles his boat against the current of the Li River

I personally thought that the Chinese had acted rightly and well. The incident was of course one of the subjects which I discussed with Vice-Premier Deng Xiaoping, and also in some talks with the Foreign Minister, Huang Hua. Huang was another earlier friend of mine from the times when he was one of Zhou Enlai's wise advisers.

Both the Ministers told me of the troubles which the Vietnamese had been causing for some time along their partly disputed frontiers; but they said candidly that these were not the main reason for their army's recent invasion of Vietnam. The principal reason was the Vietnamese military aggression against Cambodia. And they added that the purpose of the Chinese action was not to check the Vietnamese alone; the Vietnamese were operating as agents of the Russians, who should also be warned. The aggressive intrusion by Hanoi's forces into Cambodia was a part of the Moscow dictators' comprehensive plan to establish Russian "hegemony" over the whole world, by getting governments subservient to them installed in South East Asia. The Russians had been using Cuba as a similar agent in certain regions of Africa and the Middle East, where in several countries Cuban troops had aided rebellious factions to overthrow the existing governments and to install those factions – who would be lackeys of the Soviet Union – in the seats of power. Deng and Huang expressed to me criticism of the Western powers for not taking active steps to check those occurrences.

The Chinese Ministers remarked that Vietnam was "the Cuba of the Far East". And they commented that the Vietnamese would be a distinctly stronger stooge of Russia than the Cubans were. The Vietnamese population numbered about 50 million people; and their military forces of about 600,000 soldiers were extremely well trained and very modernly armed as a result of their recent long fought war against the Americans and their allies. With Soviet encouragement they had kept 200,000 of those troops in dense formation along Vietnam's border with China, where they caused frequent trouble. Moreover, with Soviet backing they had already in effect annexed Laos, and they now sought to annex Cambodia as well. No doubt their longer-term aim was to extend this pro-Soviet influence elsewhere throughout South East Asia.

Deng and Huang told me that after careful consideration the Chinese had decided to launch their "temporary and punitive" invasion of Vietnam, to teach the Vietnamese a lesson. This was to demonstrate to them that they were not invincible, and that if they tried to remain the masters of Cambodia and Laos and to extend their aggressions further afield, they would themselves be attacked – and in the end be defeated.

The Ministers said that the operation had succeeded. As a result of it the Vietnamese had withdrawn some of their divisions from Cambodia, and the Chinese had then withdrawn their troops from Vietnam as foreshadowed. Nevertheless many Vietnamese divisions still remained in Cambodia supporting the puppet administration there. The Cambodian military forces which remained loyal to the ejected government were conducting a guerrilla war against them and their puppets, and Deng expressed the view that if they received necessary material as well as moral support from friendly outside powers, they would eventually win the conflict and banish the Vietnamese from their land. Although he and his comrades in Beijing did not approve of some of the actions taken by Pol Pot's administration when it ruled in Phnom Penh, the Chinese would give them help in the form of weapons and financial aid. He hoped that the Western governments would do likewise.

He told me that the government in Beijing had now proposed that Chinese and

Vietnamese delegations should meet, to commence negotiations for a mutually satisfactory settlement of the outstanding matters of disagreement between their two governments about their common frontiers. He added emphatically that the Chinese would raise in the negotiations not only those Sino–Vietnamese border problems but also the need for the Vietnamese to withdraw from their occupations of Laos and Cambodia. He commented that if the negotiations took place they might well continue for a very long time, becoming an example of the "marathon negotiations" which had occurred in some other cases. And he added (what the Beijing government had indicated in a public statement) that if the Vietnamese remained obstinate, the Chinese reserved their right to make another punitive military invasion of Vietnam.

Deng and Huang expressed pleasure at the attitude which the members of the Association of South East Asian Nations – the Philippines, Thailand, Malaysia, Singapore and Indonesia – had adopted in condemnation of the Vietnamese act of aggression in Cambodia. Their five delegations at the United Nations meeting in New York had jointly proposed, and secured large majority support for, a resolution demanding the withdrawal of all foreign troops, both Vietnamese and Chinese, from Cambodia and Vietnam respectively. Their governments had also refused to recognize the new Cambodian regime installed by the Vietnamese. The Chinese were happy about this firm stand by those nations in the rest of South East Asia.

Deng and Huang spoke to me of their worry about some other events in other near-by parts of Asia, such as the pro-Russian "coup d'état" which had been recently engineered in Afghanistan. That was in March 1979. How right their apprehension was! Nine months later the formidable Russian military aggression against Afghanistan occurred – and peoples everywhere round the world woke up to the threat of "hegemony".

In the meantime the talks between the Chinese and the Russians about their disagreements, and the talks between the Chinese and the Vietnamese about their disputes have been making no progress. They appear to be stalled.

Some considerable problems are thus arising for the Chinese in neighbouring regions, as well as inside China itself. What will be the results of those inside China, where so much encouraging advance has been made through the last thirty years? How will developments there proceed through the next thirty years, by when its leaders hope that complete modernization will be achieved? Will the government succeed in restraining adequately the rate of growth in the country's huge population, and so be able to cope with the problems which its size provokes? If so, will it also succeed in steadily achieving its vast economic and other development aims, and so gradually further uplift the way of life of its people? Will a great majority of those people continue to support the government throughout the decades ahead during the nation's inevitably rather slow progress, or will rebellious factions gain disruptive support? And will the vast nation remain united, and continue to grow increasingly influential in international affairs?

The answers to those questions could be of crucial importance, in one way or another, to the whole of mankind. I feel optimistic about the prospect.

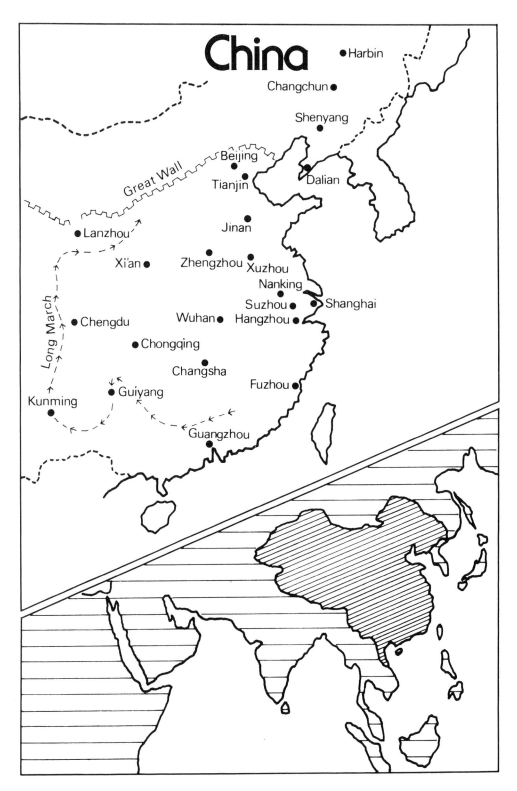

China

Harbin

Changchun

Shenyang

Great Wall

Beijing

Tianjin

Dalian

Jinan

Lanzhou

Xi'an

Zhengzhou

Xuzhou

Nanking

Long March

Suzhou

Shanghai

Chengdu

Wuhan

Hangzhou

Chongqing

Changsha

Fuzhou

Kunming

Guiyang

Guangzhou

Glossary

Index of Old and New Spellings of Names of People, Dynasties and Places

Old	*New*	*Old*	*New*
Aksai Chin	Aksayqin	Mao Tse-tung	Mao Zedong
Canton	Guangzhou	Mukden	Shenyang
Chang Hsueh-liang	Zhang Xueliang		
Chang Tso-lin	Zhang Zuolin	Nanking	Nanjing
Chiang Ching	Jiang Qing		
Chiao Kuan-hua	Qiao Guanhua	Peking	Beijing
Ch'ing	Qing	Pai Chu	Bai Zhu
Chou En-lai	Zhou Enlai		
Chungking	Chongqing	Shensi	Shaanxi
Chu Teh	Zhu De	Sian	Xian
		Soochow	Suzhou
Feng Yu-hsiang	Feng Yuxiang	Sung	Song
		Szechuan	Sichuan
Hankow	Hankou		
Han Yang	Hanyang	Tachai	Dazhai
Hua Kuo-feng	Hua Guofeng	T'ang	Tang
		Teng Hsiao-ping	Deng Xiaoping
Jehol	Chengde	Tientsin	Tianjin
		Tsing-tao	Qingdao
Kianghsi	Jiangxi		
Lin Piao	Lin Biao	Wu Chang	Wuchang
Liu Shqao-chi	Liu Shaoqi	Wu Han	Wuhan
Lung-men	Longmen	Wuhsi	Wuxi
		Yuan Shih-kai	Yuan Shikai

In some cases the old and the new spelling are the same, as in the case of Shanghai and of Chen Yi.

In other cases the old spellings, not the new, are used in the book, for historic or other reasons, such as in the cases of famous individuals who have long been dead, like some of the Emperors and Sun Yat-Sen and Chiang Kai-Shek.

Index

Technical Data

Cameras: Two Nikon F2. One Nikkormat EL.

Lenses: Nikkor Auto 20mm F/3.5, 35mm F/1.4, Micro Nikkor 55mm F/3.5, Zoom Nikkor 80–200mm F/4.5. All with lens hoods and filters.

Film stock: Kodachrome 25 and Tri-X given normal exposure at meter readings.

Flash: Three lightweight Mecablitz with mains charging units

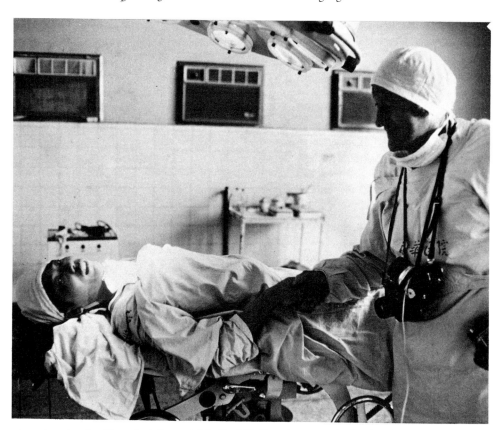

A patient in the Shanghai Second Medical College in 1973 shakes hands with William MacQuitty following the operation to remove a thyroid tumour, shown on page 106.